WHO WE ARE

A SECOND LOOK

WHO WE ARE

A SECOND LOOK

Margaret Gibelman
Philip H. Schervish

NASW PRESS

NATIONAL ASSOCIATION OF SOCIAL WORKERS
Washington, DC

Jay J. Cayner, ACSW, LSW, *President*
Josephine Nieves, MSW, PhD, *Executive Director*

Linda Beebe, *Executive Editor*
Nancy A. Winchester, *Editorial Services Director*
Fran Pflieger, Maben Publications, Inc., *Copy Editor*
Louise Goines, *Proofreader*
Susan J. Harris, *Proofreader*
Bernice Eisen, *Indexer*

Library of Congress Cataloging-in-Publication Data
Gibelman, Margaret.
    Who we are : a second look / Margaret Gibelman, Philip H. Schervish. — 2nd ed.
    p.   cm.
    Includes bibliographical references and index.
    ISBN 0-87101-261-8 (alk. paper)
    1. Social workers—United States—Statistics. 2. National Association of Social Workers—Membership—Statistics.
I. Schervish, Philip H. II. Title.
HV40.8.U6G53 1996
331.7'613613'0973—dc21   96-29546
                                                   CIP

Printed in the United States of America

CONTENTS

FIGURES

TABLES

Tables

PREFACE

—

Included among the purposes of the National Association of Social Workers, an organization of 155,000 professional social workers, is "to assume responsibility for man- and woman-power planning and development for the range of personnel—professional, technical, and supporting—needed in the provision of social services." The professional labor force is the vehicle through which social work can

- ensure the quality and effectiveness of social work practice in the United States through services to individuals, groups, and communities
- improve the conditions of life in this democratic society
- work in unity to maintain and promote high standards of practice and of preparation for practice with the goal of alleviating or preventing sources of deprivation, distress, and strain (*Bylaws of the National Association of Social Workers*, as amended, 1990).

The achievement of these aims is predicated on the existence of a professional labor force to carry out the profession's mission. Relatively little attention, however, has been paid to the question of the composition of the social work labor force. Knowledge about "who we are" enables us to assess the characteristics of our labor force relative to our mandate. Furthermore, information about who we are forms the basis and allows for the exploration of "where we are going." Addressing both issues is critical to the continued growth and development of any profession.

This book provides answers to the first question through the study of a large subset of the social work population—the NASW membership. With the 1993 publication of *Who We Are: The Social Work Labor Force as Reflected in the NASW Membership*, NASW took a major step to examine the demographic and employment characteristics of this large segment of the social work population. This second edition identifies changes occurring within the social work labor force and sets forth a continuing agenda by which to identify and debate not only where the profession is headed but also the extent to which current and future directions are consistent with a consensus definition of where we *should* be headed.

We first became interested in the topic of the social work labor force when we began to notice changes in the composition of the social work student body—younger, fewer males, fewer people of color, with primary interest in clinical practice and intentions to enter independent social work practice. The shift, in our experience, was gradual but distinct. Were we seeing a phenomenon unique only to one geographic area or was this evidence of larger trends within the current and future professional labor force? A close look at the data suggests that there are, indeed, significant trends taking shape within the professional social work labor force.

Trend data on the social work labor force provide an important base for formulating labor force development strategies. These data can be used, for example, to help formulate professional standards, determine criteria for competence certification, and adapt social work education curricula to ensure the existence of a professional labor force equipped with the knowledge and skills needed to respond to and lead in meeting future human services needs. A fundamental premise is that the professional labor force should and must evolve within the context of a changing society and emerging social needs.

It is our continued hope that this volume, in revealing with some degree of clarity "who we are," keeps open and encourages the debate about the nature of the professional labor force—what it is and what it should be.

Any undertaking of this type is not accomplished alone. First, acknowledgment and thanks are extended to the thousands of NASW members who, each year, take the time to update the demographic data questions on their membership renewal form. The data reported here are accurate in the aggregate only to the extent that members take the extra few minutes to update their records.

We would also like to acknowledge the work of Linda Beebe and members of the NASW staff in identifying the need for a periodic analysis of the social work labor force, as reflected in the NASW membership, and affording resources to this endeavor, providing access to the data, and offering encouragement and assistance from beginning to end. The careful review of the drafts and intellectual contributions of staff are very much appreciated. Former executive directors Sheldon Goldstein and Robert Cohen both expressed enthusiastic willingness to

Preface

seriously address the issues raised by this study, ranging from internal data-collection procedures to defining a long-range agenda for the association. Fran Pflieger provided able and thoughtful editorial assistance, and Nancy Winchester expedited the production process.

A special thank you goes to Peg, Anice, and Katie Schervish and to Steve Kraft for their support and encouragement. Appreciation is also extended to our colleagues at Yeshiva University, Wurzweiler School of Social Work, and Howard University, School of Social Work.

CHAPTER 1

THE EVOLVING SOCIAL WORK
LABOR FORCE

The average NASW member received a master's degree in social
work sometime during the past nine years; earns $7,350 a year; and
is a caseworker in a federal, state, or municipal governmental
agency. (Becker, 1961, p. 2)

These were among the findings of the National Association of Social
Workers's (NASW's) first survey of members' salaries and employment.
The results of the 1961 study and the periodic surveys that have been
conducted in ensuing years provide a historical perspective by which to
contrast this most recent analysis of data on NASW's membership.

Who We Are: A Second Look reports on the characteristics of social
workers who are members of NASW. Membership in NASW is voluntary, and thus the sample is self-selected. The information was drawn
from the self-reports of NASW members who completed demographic
profiles as part of their application to join the association and updated
the same information each year on their membership renewal form.

The first report of the salaries and characteristics of NASW members
was completed in 1961 (Becker, 1961). Reference to a 1982 report,
using 1982 information, appeared in an article detailing shifts in
practice published in the *NASW News* ("Membership Survey," 1983).

NASW's 1987 salary study included information on then-current
salaries and employment characteristics of NASW members in an effort
to "examine how these salaries compare with those paid to the members
of other selected professions" (NASW, 1987, p. 1). The report was the
first effort to build a database on social work practice and salaries; to
publish reports needed by practitioners, administrators, and educators;

and to provide a base for periodically updating recommendations about minimum annual salaries. The computerization of the membership records made such comprehensive studies possible.

Unfortunately, the 1987 report provides only a partial base for later comparative analyses, because the profile questions completed by members failed to distinguish between those employed full-time and those working part-time. This weakness in the data collection form was rectified, and beginning with the 1988 membership year comparative analyses became possible.

In 1993, NASW published *Who We Are: The Social Work Labor Force as Reflected in the NASW Membership* (Gibelman & Schervish, 1993), which provided a profile of the demographics and practice (function, setting, and area) of the NASW membership based on the full data set of members for 1988 and 1991. Comparisons between 1988 and 1991 were facilitated by the use of the same demographic profile form in both years. NASW modified the data collection form in 1994, but in this process made every effort to ensure that patterns and trends could still be discerned over time, using 1988 as the base year.

In this second edition of *Who We Are,* the data set comprises the full NASW membership as of June 30, 1995. Data from the Bureau of Labor Statistics (BLS) of the U.S. Department of Labor are also reported, when applicable, to compare the characteristics of NASW members with the demographics of the larger labor force in social welfare.

PURPOSES AND USES OF THIS VOLUME

Part of the professional social worker's job is to consistently interpret for the public who we are, what we do, and the nature of the populations we serve. In this respect, hard facts about the social work labor force serve an important public education purpose.

At a time when Congress and state legislatures are grappling with hard budget decisions and the future of human services funding and programs is being debated, the ability to interpret who we are and what we do is especially important. Several questions are consistently posed by policymakers, representatives of federal agencies, administrators of social services and mental health agencies, social work educators, individual social workers (including NASW members), and the association:

- What are the characteristics of professional social workers who are members of NASW?

- How have such characteristics changed over time?
- Where do NASW members work, and what functions do they perform?
- How much money do they earn?
- What factors affect their earning capacity?
- What social problems do social workers address?
- What populations do they serve?
- How do the demographics of the membership reflect the changing nature of the social work profession and social work practice?

Answers to these questions allow for an increased understanding of the composition and characteristics of the large proportion of the social work labor force who are members of NASW. They also establish a base for formulating some key policy issues for professional debate. These issues include a consideration of what NASW members do (the functions they perform) versus what the profession and NASW believe and advocate that they do and should be doing; how the practice settings and auspices in which NASW members work and the functions performed by them fit with conventional wisdom about these aspects of social work practice; and how NASW's priorities, standards, objectives, and programs relate to and reflect the demographic realities of the association's membership.

Many audiences will find this updated information about a subset of the total social work labor force useful. Planners and policymakers can apply the findings to verify or debate assumptions about the social work labor force and to identify new policy and practice issues for the profession. Researchers can compare the findings with data available about other professions and with statistics on social work education to identify key variables that affect recruitment and retention not only in NASW but in the social work profession as a whole. Social work educators will find the data valuable in discussions of curriculum reform and course development. Boards of directors and administrators of social welfare organizations and agencies can use this information to inform deliberations on personnel management, recruitment, retention, and compensation. Individual social workers can use it to re-examine their own career development and future plans in relation to both other practitioners and professional standards. Finally, comparative salary data provide a practical framework for negotiating individual and group employment contracts.

Although this book cites some of the professional literature produced by NASW and other sources, the purpose of such references is to high-light consistencies and disparities among past research, conventional professional theory and wisdom, and statistical findings regarding the demographics and characteristics of NASW members in 1995. Therefore, no attempt was made to conduct an extensive literature search. Rather, consistent with the first edition, the goal was to present findings based on the self-reports of NASW members that expand knowledge of the characteristics of this group of social workers.

NASW MEMBERS IN RELATION TO ALL SOCIAL WORKERS

The *NASW Bylaws* detail three classes of membership—regular, associate, and student—and allow additional classes to be established by the Delegate Assembly (NASW, 1994).

Regular membership is limited to social workers who have received an undergraduate or graduate degree from a program accredited or recognized by the Council on Social Work Education (CSWE). *Associate membership* is limited to those who are employed in a social work capacity as determined by the Board of Directors (excluding self-employed practitioners or those in a private group practice) who have an accredited baccalaureate degree in a field other than social work; there are some limitations on membership privileges afforded to associate members. *Student membership* is open to students currently enrolled in a CSWE-accredited social work degree program or a program approved for candidacy; the dues rate for student members is less than that for regular or associate members. In addition, members who join as students pay a transitional dues rate for the first two years after graduation.

In keeping with the provisions of the *Bylaws,* additional membership categories appear on the NASW membership application form. The categories of retired, unemployed, and doctoral candidate membership are open to individuals who are eligible for regular membership and are retired or unemployed and unsalaried in any field and to doctoral candidates in social work education programs; this group also pays a reduced dues rate.

Although NASW is the largest organization of professional social workers, heretofore its membership constituted an undetermined proportion of the total social work population in the United States who meet the criteria for eligibility. BLS (1991) estimated that the total social work labor force, composed of those holding the title of social worker, was 603,000 in 1991. By 1994, that number had grown to 666,000 (BLS, 1994).

The first NASW demographic study of its membership (Becker, 1961) coincided with a BLS study (1961) on social welfare personnel. The BLS study included in its analysis selected positions in health,

4

recreation, and welfare agencies. According to Becker, "the list of job titles in the BLS study contained positions that would fall within the NASW Working Definition of Social Work Practice as well as those which might not fall within the definition" (p. 2). Furthermore, people who were eligible and not eligible for NASW membership were included in the BLS data set.

Using the broader category of social welfare, rather than social work personnel, the BLS definition, exclusive of recreation workers, was estimated at 105,000 during the summer of 1960. In March 1961, there were 28,000 NASW members, 22,000 of whom were employed. Thus, Becker (1961) estimated that in 1961, 21 percent of all people in the social welfare field were NASW members.

It is now possible to derive more accurate proportional estimates of the NASW membership relative to the total social welfare labor force. In 1994, for the first time, BLS included as a subset of the occupational category of social work the degree held by individuals in that category. Prior to 1994, the BLS category of social work included all those who identified themselves as holding a social work position but did not attempt to attach any form of credentials to the respondents. By including the degrees held, the 1994 BLS occupational data offer a significantly more accurate picture of the total social work labor force.

As of June 30, 1995, there were 153,814 NASW members. Although comparisons of 1994 BLS statistics and 1995 NASW membership figures are inexact, they do provide a rough estimate of the proportion of NASW members to all social workers in the United States. Of the 666,000 social and human services workers in the 1994 BLS study, 484,000 were classified as social workers. Of those, 289,000 held a bachelor's degree, 175,000 held a master's degree, and 8,000 held a doctoral degree. These figures suggest that the NASW membership constitutes approximately 32 percent of the total social work labor force.

Every two years since 1957, BLS has developed long-term (eight- to 15-year) projections of the likely employment conditions for each occupational group for which it maintains data (BLS, 1993). In 1992, on the basis of current labor force size, aggregate economy, interindustry relationships, and related factors, BLS projected that by the year 2005 the number of people employed in social work and holding a social work degree would range from a low of 645,000 to a high of 693,000 (BLS, 1993).

Unfortunately, few studies have investigated why some professional social workers choose to join NASW and others do not. Financial considerations, the cost versus the perceived benefits of affiliation, identification with other primary reference groups, lack of information about NASW and its membership benefits, lack of interest in affiliation with membership organizations, or disagreement with the purposes or programs of NASW may be among the reasons some social workers do not join the professional association.

An earlier study conducted by Westat (1984), under contract to NASW, explored the attitudes of 1,205 NASW members, lapsed members, and nonmembers about NASW's current programs and services, reasons for not joining NASW or continuing membership, and expectations related to the decision to join professional associations such as NASW. The differences in the characteristics of the three groups were as follows:

- A higher proportion of NASW members than of lapsed members and nonmembers were employed in the mental health field.
- A higher proportion of nonmembers than of members or lapsed members were employed in the fields of corrections and public welfare.
- A higher proportion of lapsed members and nonmembers than of members were government employees, and proportionally fewer social workers in these two groups worked in the private for-profit sector.

The Westat report also concluded that NASW members, but not lapsed members and nonmembers, were likely to belong to more than one professional association.

A 1995 membership needs assessment conducted by NASW of a sample of 3,985 members also sheds some light on why a sizable proportion of social workers choose not to affiliate with their professional association (AWP Research, 1995). The results of this study pointed to the diversity of the profession and the range of interests of its labor force, a fact that suggests that not all members' needs can be met through one association. The divergent interests of social workers may mean that no one organization can appeal to the totality of the professional labor force.

CONTEXT OF SOCIAL WORK PRACTICE

There are many assumptions about who social workers are and what they do, and the profession's definitions of itself and of the boundaries of social work practice are both fluid. Debates about social workers and their roles have been waged since the earliest days of the profession. In the early 1900s, Flexner (1915) questioned whether social work was a profession and Richmond (1917) sought to identify the skills required for work with individuals and families. CSWE's 1959 Curriculum Study (Boehm, 1959) pointed to "the lack of a single, widely recognized, or generally accepted statement . . . of the aims and purposes of social work" (p. 40). This landmark study concluded that the core activities of social work have not been authoritatively differentiated. In 1973, NASW sought to explicate levels of practice and to develop a classification structure through the promulgation of *Standards for Social Service Manpower* (NASW, 1973). Refinements of definitions and concepts were incorporated in *Standards for the Classification of Social Work Practice* (NASW, 1981).

Certain themes reverberate throughout the years in regard to the boundaries of the social work profession. These themes include ongoing debates within the profession about the appropriate emphasis on social work on behalf of all people versus a focus on special population groups or special social problems; the application of diverse theoretical orientations by which to understand people and guide interventions with them and on their behalf; the choice of methods of practice; the role and place of generalist and specialist practitioners; and the role of social work in certain areas of service, such as public welfare (Minahan, 1982). The relative emphasis given to these areas of debate are frequently defined by the prevailing cultural, political, social, and organizational environment. Within this context, social work has also been described as "a residual institution with boundless areas of concern" (Bar-On, 1994, p. 53).

Social work's sanction comes from the society of which it is a part. This implies that society recognizes that there are disparities between "what is" and "what should be" and that there is a need to rectify this condition (Rosenfeld, 1983). The degree to which society is willing to identify such incongruities depends on the sociopolitical context of the times. Any attempt to "fix" the boundaries of the profession is likely to be unsuccessful, given the constantly changing societal environment and prevailing ideologies. Thus, the domain of social work today is likely to be somewhat different tomorrow; it is a dynamic and evolving profession (Gibelman, 1995). The evolution of the profession is also rooted in changing technology and intervention methodology. Our knowledge base continues to grow. Theories are subject to more rigorous testing.

Changes in the definition of the profession and the characteristics of professional practice reflect the evolving and dynamic nature of social work. Hopps and Pinderhughes (1987) saw such changes as positive:

"Because social work continues to be seen as emerging and developing, it is important that the profession constantly defines and clarifies itself over the years" (p. 352). These changes can be stimulated by internal or external forces (Walz & Groze, 1991). The 1960s War on Poverty is an example of externally driven change. Although social work theory and practice have always included an advocacy component, the War on Poverty provided an unprecedented opportunity to recruit into the profession and provide job opportunities for those wishing to practice advocacy as a primary function (Gibelman, 1995).

"Reaganomics" posed a new set of challenges for the profession of social work. In the early years of the first Reagan administration, the social work literature reflected concern about the potential impact of the president's agenda, an agenda that echoes today. Social workers were urged to adapt. Austin (1984) argued that managing cutbacks involved new role requirements for agency administrators, including strategic planning and "cheerleading" (for example, increasing staff involvement in all levels of decision making).

The current Republican political agenda seeks to reduce the scope and role of government; return a greater share of decision-making responsibility to the states; reduce the deficit; and, in the process, decrease funding for societal "safety net" programs, including Aid to Families with Dependent Children, Medicare, and Medicaid. This agenda and the countervailing forces constitute the parameters in which social welfare policy decisions will be made now and in the foreseeable future; they affect the breadth, content, and form of the programs and services for which social workers are responsible (Dear, 1995).

But as in other eras in which social welfare funding and programming was constricted, the adage "what goes around comes around" seems a likely scenario. Some forecast that as social needs go unattended, a pent-up demand for services will develop in the long run ("Social Work Deans," 1995). The likely result is a resurgence of social services and increased employment opportunities for social workers.

The substantial change in social workers' functions over the history of the profession relates to social work's integral relationship with society. The traditional emphasis on practical problems, concrete tasks, and the provision of resources has changed to a focus on more clinical concerns—in other words, from "hard" social work functions to "soft" ones (Davis, 1988). This current focus on clinical social work is evident in the growing proportion of social workers in private, psychotherapeutically oriented practice, as detailed in chapter 5. However, pending legislative changes and the growth of a managed health care system suggest that the pendulum may well swing back to emphasize the more concrete services.

Social workers continue to influence their environment, not just respond to it. For example, during the 1960s social workers successfully pressed state legislatures to enact consumer choice legislation, which recognizes social workers as qualified providers of mental health services and makes them eligible for insurance and other third-party reimbursement (Whiting, 1995). These laws stipulate that consumers have the freedom to choose any qualified mental health provider, of which social workers are one category, if the consumer's health insurance provides mental health coverage (Whiting, 1995). As a precursor to such legislation, social workers were also successful in gaining legal recognition in the form of licensing and registration laws, now operative in all states and the District of Columbia. Legal regulation of social work is almost always a requirement for eligibility under state consumer choice or vendorship laws (Whiting, 1995).

Social work has also been the beneficiary of public policy, which has helped expand the boundaries of social work practice. The Omnibus Budget Reconciliation Act of 1989 included a provision for clinical social workers to join the limited class of mental health professionals who are eligible for reimbursement under Medicare. And, more recently, final regulations for the Family and Medical Leave Act of 1993 include clinical social workers as health care providers. Clinical social workers were added to the definition of "health care providers" following active lobbying by more than 400 practicing social workers, five members of Congress, and 14 organizations ("Family Leave Regs," 1995).

Many federal policies that have expanded the boundaries of social work's domain concern the establishment of policies and programs to meet the needs of specific populations (Gibelman, 1995). In these instances, social workers are responsible, in whole or part, for planning, implementing, and administering the programs. For example, new and expanding roles for social workers resulted from the enactment of such national social welfare policies as the McKinney Homeless Assistance Act of 1987, which was the first major federal initiative that approached the problem of homelessness from a multiple problem framework; the Adoption Assistance and Child Welfare Act of 1980, which ushered in an emphasis on permanency planning and family preservation; the Americans with Disabilities Act of 1990; and the Anti-Drug Abuse Act of 1988. These and other laws provided a new conceptualization of social problems and the financial incentive for new programs.

9

.

Change comes from both the preferences of the professional social work labor force and the response of social workers to external change. At various times in recent history, this societal context has served as a stimulus to expand professional boundaries; at other times, social workers have had to advocate for and create opportunities in spite of prevailing politics and ideology. Today, the context of professional practice is affected by fiscal constraints and growing social ills (Hopps & Collins, 1995).

The existence of human need remains constant, and although social work roles and functions may shift, the profession remains rooted in American society (Gibelman, 1995). Stewart's (1984) commentary on the future of the profession, written during the Reagan era, holds true today:

> Social work, a growth profession, has an important future in this nation. It is precisely social work's diagnostic and practice orientation, its focus on persons in relation to their environments, that makes its knowledge and skills so vital today. Our people are experiencing major disruptions and displacements because of revolutionary and public social policy changes. Inherent in those changes is an increased need for professionals best equipped to help persons cope with significant shifts in their lives and environments. That is social work's forte. (p. 2)

DEFINITION OF SOCIAL WORK PRACTICE

Virtually all professions include specialties within their professional training and practice. The legal profession, for example, includes members who are specialists in tax, criminal, or family law. Medicine, of course, has a wide range of specialty areas, such as dermatology and psychiatry. Social work is equally complex and broad.

As the profession has evolved, the definitions of the profession and its practice have been subject to periodic debate, re-examination, and change. As a profession that interrelates with and seeks to influence the larger socioeconomic and political environment, it is not surprising that the definition of social work is dynamic, rather than rigid and static.

The intent of NASW's *Standards for the Classification of Social Work Practice* (NASW, 1981) was "to identify the specific social work content of social service employment and to provide a basis for differentiating among levels of practice" (p. 3). The document defines social work practice as consisting of professionally responsible intervention to (1) enhance the developmental, problem-solving, and coping capacities of people; (2) promote the effective and humane operation of systems that provide resources and services to people; (3) link people with systems that provide them with resources, services, and opportunities; and (4) contribute to the development and improvement of social policy.

Interventions are provided to individuals, families, small groups, organizations, neighborhoods, and communities. They involve the disciplined application of knowledge and skill to a broad range of problems that affect the well-being of people, both directly and indirectly. They are carried out at differentiated levels of knowledge and skill through an organized network of professional social workers within the boundaries of ethical norms established by the profession and the sanction of society. Within these norms, the interventions may be carried out in cooperation with other helping disciplines and organizations as part of any human services enterprise (NASW, 1981).

Social workers provide services in a wide variety of settings and at all functional levels of practice. For example, they deliver services in private practice, institutions, hospitals, school systems, clinics or centers, and correctional facilities. Social workers function in direct service, supervision, management, policy development, research, community organization, and education–training capacities. In diverse practice settings, they carry out a series of functions, each of which is composed of a set of distinctive tasks. The relationship between the goals of social work practice and the functions and tasks involved is illustrated in Table 1.1.

SOURCE AND CHARACTERISTICS OF THE DATA

The NASW membership application form asks prospective members to provide basic demographic and professional background data, which are entered into the association's database. Each year, as part of the membership renewal process, members are asked to update the information on file.

Data about the characteristics of NASW members were drawn from the information members provided on the application or renewal forms. They were extracted for analysis on July 1, 1995, and include all members whose status was current on that date. In the first edition of this volume, data from 1988 and 1991 were compared; at that time, 1991 constituted the most recent data and 1988 was selected as a

TABLE 1.1

Summary of Social Work Functions

Goal	Function
To enhance the problem-solving, coping, and developmental capacities of people	Assessment Diagnosis Detection–Identification Support–Assistance Advice–Counseling Advocacy–Enabling
To link people with systems that provide resources, services, and opportunities	Referral Organizing Mobilization Negotiation Exchange
To promote effective and humane operations of systems	Administration–Management Program development Supervision Coordination Consultation Evaluation Staff development
To develop and improve social policy	Policy analysis Planning Policy development Reviewing Policy advocacy

Source: Adapted from National Association of Social Workers. (1981). *NASW standards for the classification of social work practice* (pp. 12–16). Silver Spring, MD: National Association of Social Workers.

comparison year because it was the first year in which NASW maintained the complete data set in a format comparable to what is now being used. The year 1988 thus provides an initial base from which to monitor changes and trends over time.

In 1994, NASW introduced a new membership application form; the changes in the form were also reflected in a new member demographic form sent with each member's renewal notice. (See appendix 1 for a copy of the form used prior to 1994 and the new form introduced in 1994.) The need for a new data collection form was highlighted, in part, by problems that became apparent in the analysis of data conducted for the first edition of *Who We Are*.

The characteristics included in the analysis were derived from the following data[1]:

Variable	Item
Residence	State and zip code
Highest social work degree held	BSW, MSW, DSW, or PhD
Date of highest social work degree	Year
Ethnic–racial group	Native American, Asian or Pacific Islander, African American–Black, Chicano–Mexican American, Other Hispanic–Latino, White–Caucasian, mixed heritage, other
Major field of practice (primary and, as applicable, secondary employment)	Aging, child–family welfare, criminal justice, medical–health care, mental health, occupational, other
Major function (primary and, as applicable, secondary employment)	Administration–management, clinical–direct practice, community organization–advocacy, policy analysis–development, research, supervision, teaching, training, other

(continued)

_____

[1] Social workers may be employed in more than one job and one practice setting. For example, a social worker may work half-time for a family services agency and maintain a private clinical practice. Or a social worker may be employed by a university to teach mental health practice but perform consultation or research for another agency or in independent practice. Observations about these combinations are made later in this book.

Work setting (primary and, as applicable, secondary employment)	Business–industry, colleges–universities, courts–justice system, health—inpatient, health—outpatient, managed care, mental health—inpatient, mental health—outpatient, private practice—group, private practice—solo, residential facility, school (preschool to grade 12), social services agency, other
Type of organization (primary and, as applicable, secondary employment)	Public, local, state, federal—military; federal—nonmilitary; private nonprofit, private for-profit
Work focus (primary and, as applicable, secondary employment)	Alcohol–drugs, disabilities, employment related, family issues, grief–bereavement, health, housing, income maintenance, individual–behavior, international, violence–victim assistance, other
Current annual income (primary and secondary employment)	Full- or part-time
Total years of social work experience	Years
Academy of Certified Social Workers (ACSW) status	Yes or no
Approximate number of clients served per year	_____
Ever held public office	Yes or no

All categories of members except associate members (those employed in social work capacities but holding a degree in a field other than social work) are included in the membership profile presented in chapter 2. For the more detailed analyses in later chapters, international, retired–unemployed, and student members are excluded, in the interest of including in the data set only those whose status, positions, and salary are the most comparable. In most analyses, BSW, MSW, and PhD–DSW members are analyzed separately.

LIMITATIONS OF THE DATA

The study population is limited to NASW members. Although BLS is now reporting occupational data on social workers on the basis of degree rather than position title, we still know very little about the larger population of social workers in the United States. Furthermore, it is not known whether the characteristics of social workers who choose to join NASW differ from those who choose not to join.

An additional limitation is the currency of the information on NASW members, also a concern in the first edition of *Who We Are*. Although membership is renewed each year, not all members update their profile information on the demographic data form, and some do not complete all the questions. Therefore, a relatively large proportion of the data are missing. A related problem is that when a member updates only part of his or her profile, information is retained from the member's earlier responses to those questions for which no new responses are provided. Thus, for example, in 1995 a member may have updated information about employment auspice, but not about salary. Therefore, the old salary figure (from the last time the member responded to the salary question) would appear as part of the updated record.

NASW includes the demographic data form with the first membership renewal sent to each member. However, the demographic data form is not included in follow-up billings. Thus, members who do not pay their dues in response to the first renewal notice and do not retain the demographic form for later response are not able to provide updated information. NASW is now exploring the feasibility of including the demographic data form in follow-up renewal notices.

Another limitation noted in the first edition of *Who We Are* was that of terminology. At that time, it was noted that the terminology used on the demographic questionnaire—such as field of practice, specialization, practice setting, and auspice—may not be commonly understood by NASW members. Variations in the number of respondents from question to question suggested that the distinctions among practice area, practice setting, and auspice of practice were not readily understood and that respondents only answered when they were reasonably sure of the intent of the question. This misunderstanding would account, in part, for variations in the number of responses by item. Many of these terminology problems have been addressed in the revised demographic questionnaire. However, there continues to be a substantial variation in response rate by question.

Because of the limitations of the database, information is not available about the precise nature of the work of social workers engaged in social work practice. Similarly, it is not possible to report on the characteristics of social work clients–patients. Readers are, however, referred to Teare and Sheafor's (1995) analysis of social work practice and practitioners. The authors conducted cluster and factor analysis on aggregate data collected in three separate studies done between 1983 and 1990 from a sample of 7,000 social workers. The analyses yielded information on 131 discrete tasks that were organized into broader descriptive categories to describe the practice of social work.

Given the stated limitations of the NASW data, any generalizations to all social workers in the United States must be made with extreme caution.

ANALYSIS OF THE DATA

The NASW membership database included 153,814 members on June 30, 1995. The entire data set was used to establish a membership profile, which is presented in chapter 2. For analyses in chapters 3 through 5, a subset of the total membership database was created to represent social workers who are currently employed full- or part-time. Chapter 6, which reports on the salaries of NASW members, includes a subset of employed full-time members.

Using the Statistical Package for the Social Sciences (SPSS), the authors conducted frequencies and cross-tabulations for each variable in the NASW membership application–renewal form (see appendix 1). The results of the frequencies and cross-tabulations were used in the descriptions and accompanying narrative interpretations of NASW members. Throughout this volume, comparisons are made between 1995 data and earlier findings reported in the first edition of *Who We Are* for the years 1988 and 1991.

REFERENCES

Austin, M. J. (1984). Managing cutbacks in the 1980s. *Social Work, 29,* 428–434.

AWP Research. (1995). *NASW membership needs assessment survey.* Washington, DC: Author.

Bar-On, AA. (1994). The elusive boundaries of social work. *Journal of Sociology & Social Welfare, 21*(3), 53–67.

Becker, R. (1961). *Study of salaries of NASW members.* New York: National Association of Social Workers.

Boehm, W. (1959). *Objectives of the social work curriculum of the future* (Social Work Curriculum Study, Vol. 1). New York: Council on Social Work Education.

Bureau of Labor Statistics. (1961). *Salaries and working conditions of social welfare manpower in 1960.* New York: National Social Welfare Assembly.

Bureau of Labor Statistics. (1991). *Household data survey: Employed civilians by detailed occupation, 1983–1991.* Washington, DC: Author.

Bureau of Labor Statistics. (1993, Spring). *Occupational outlook quarterly, 1992–2005.* Washington, DC: Author.

Bureau of Labor Statistics. (1994, January). *Employment and earnings.* Washington, DC: Author.

Davis, S. (1988). "Soft" versus "hard" social work. *Social Work, 33,* 373–374.

Dear, R. N. (1995). Social welfare policy. In R. L. Edwards (Ed.-in-Chief), *Encyclopedia of social work* (19th ed., Vol. 3, pp. 2226–2237). Washington, DC: NASW Press.

Family-leave regs revision adds clinicians. (1995, February). *NASW News,* p. 1.

Flexner, A. (1915). Is social work a profession? In *Proceedings of the National Conference of Charities and Corrections* (pp. 576–590). Chicago: Hildman Printing Co.

Gibelman, M. (1995). *What social workers do.* Washington, DC: NASW Press.

Gibelman, M., & Schervish, P. (1993). *Who we are: The social work labor force as reflected in the NASW membership.* Washington, DC: NASW Press.

Hopps, J. G., & Collins, P. M. (1995). Social work profession overview. In R. L. Edwards (Ed.-in-Chief), *Encyclopedia of social work* (19th ed., Vol. 3, pp. 2266–2282). Washington, DC: NASW Press.

Hopps, J. G., & Pinderhughes, E. (1987). Profession of social work: Contemporary characteristics. In A. Minahan (Ed.-in-Chief), *Encyclopedia of social work* (18th ed., Vol. 2, pp. 351–365). Silver Spring, MD: National Association of Social Workers.

Membership survey shows practice shifts. (1983, November). *NASW News,* pp. 6, 7.

Minahan, A. (1982). It was the best of times, it was the worst of times [Editorial]. *Social Work, 27,* 291.

National Association of Social Workers. (1973). *Standards for social service manpower.* Silver Spring, MD: Author.

National Association of Social Workers. (1981). *NASW standards for the classification of social work practice*. Silver Spring, MD: Author.

National Association of Social Workers. (1987). *Salaries in social work: A summary report on the salaries of NASW members*, July 1986, June 1987. Silver Spring, MD: Author.

National Association of Social Workers. (1994). *Bylaws of the National Association of Social Workers*. Washington, DC: Author.

Richmond, M. (1917). *Social diagnosis*. New York: Russell Sage Foundation.

Rosenfeld, J. M. (1983). The domain and expertise of social work: A conceptualization. *Social Work, 28,* 186–191.

Social work deans: A commentary on profound change and its meaning for the profession. (1995, January). *Currents,* pp. 1, 5.

Stewart, R. (1984, March). From the president. *NASW News,* p. 2.

Teare, R. J., & Sheafor, B. W. (1995). *Practice-sensitive social work education.* Alexandria, VA: Council on Social Work Education.

Walz, T., & Groze, V. (1991). The mission of social work revisited: An agenda for the 1990s. *Social Work, 36,* 500–504.

Westat. (1984). *A study of attitudes of NASW members, lapsed members and non-members*. Rockville, MD: Author.

Whiting, L. (1995). Vendorship. In R. L. Edwards (Ed.-in-Chief), *Encyclopedia of social work* (19th ed., Vol. 3, pp. 2427–2431). Washington, DC: NASW Press.

CHAPTER 2

DEMOGRAPHIC OVERVIEW OF THE NASW MEMBERSHIP
━━━

This chapter presents a profile of all categories of NASW members in 1995 and compares it with the profile of members in 1988 and 1991. Because this overview includes data on students, data related to income have been omitted here; findings would be skewed in a negative direction and would not accurately reflect salary ranges. The income of full-time employed NASW members is discussed in chapter 6.

NASW MEMBERSHIP

From 1991 to 1995, the NASW membership grew from 134,250 to 153,814, or 15 percent, the same percentage growth achieved between 1988 and 1991. As noted in chapter 1, these numbers do not reflect the total number of social workers practicing in the United States. According to BLS (1995), there were 484,000 employees who held the title of social worker and had a degree in social work (BSW or MSW) in 1992, the first and the most recent year for which data are available. BLS also provides an annual tally of the working population by occupational title, exclusive of information about specific social work degree. People in these positions may or may not hold social work degrees or fit the NASW definition of a professional social worker. In 1994, 666,000 employees occupied social work–titled positions, up 10 percent from 603,000 in 1991. The profession's rate of growth seems to be slower than that of NASW (see Figure 2.1).

GENDER

The NASW membership continues to be overwhelmingly female. In 1995, 79.4 percent (119,840) of the 150,982 members responding to

F!GURE 2.1

Number of NASW Members versus BLS Counts of Human Services
Workers and Social Workers

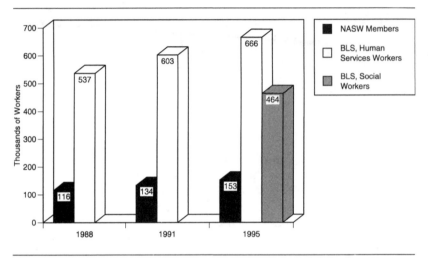

Note: BLS = Bureau of Labor Statistics. The first year BLS collected data on position by
degree was 1995.

this question were women. The proportion of women in the membership continues to increase. In 1988, 74.9 percent of responding members were women; in 1991, the proportion of women increased to 77.3
percent of responding members (see Figure 2.2).

The difference between the genders in the BLS survey was not as
great as in the NASW figures, although both sets of data show an
increase in the proportion of women. BLS reported that women constituted 69.3 percent of those occupying social work–titled positions in
1994, up from 68.0 percent in 1991 and 66.0 percent in 1988.

ETHNICITY

Data related to the ethnicity of NASW members reveal a consistent
pattern across the three study years. Of the 113,222 members who
indicated their ethnicity in 1995, 87.9 percent (99,502) were white,
down slightly as a proportion of total membership. In 1991, 88.1
percent of respondents were white and in 1988, 88.4 percent of respondents were white. African Americans were the second largest ethnic
group in the membership, at 5.7 percent (6,443) in 1995, 5.9 percent in

FIGURE 2.2

Percentage of NASW Members, by Gender

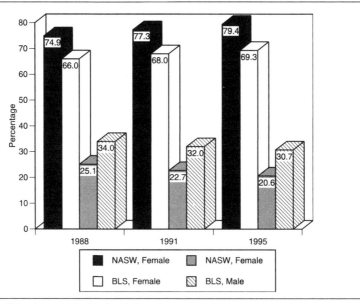

Note: BLS = Bureau of Labor Statistics.

1991, and 5.7 percent in 1988. In 1995, Asians made up 1.8 percent (2,060) of the membership, up slightly from 1991 (1.5 percent) and 1988 (1.5 percent). Native Americans constituted 0.6 percent (624) of the membership in 1995, up slightly from 0.5 in 1991 and 1988. Hispanics, including Chicanos, Puerto Ricans, and other Hispanics, constituted 2.8 percent (3,129) of the membership in 1995, again up slightly from 2.6 percent in 1991 and 2.4 percent in 1988. Members of mixed heritage made up 1.2 percent (1,393) of the membership in 1995, down slightly from 1.4 percent for the category "other" in both 1988 and 1991 (see Table 2.1).

BLS occupational data for those occupying social work–titled positions are more positive in regard to ethnic diversity. For 1994, BLS (1995) reported that about 72.4 percent (482,000) of those holding social work–titled positions were white, 24.1 percent (160,000) were black, 7 percent (47,000) were Hispanic, and 1 percent (7,000) were "other." The BLS statistics for those holding a social work degree did not include a breakdown by ethnicity.

21

TABLE 2.1

Ethnicity of NASW Members

Ethnicity	1988 n	1988 %	1991 n	1991 %	1995 n	1995 %	Percentage Change 1988– 1995
African American	5,254	5.7	6,690	5.9	6,443	5.7	0.0
Asian	1,427	1.5	1,751	1.5	2,060	1.8	0.3
Hispanic	2,206	2.4	3,002	2.6	3,129	2.8	0.4
Mixed heritage[a]					1,393	1.2	N/A[b]
Native American	463	0.5	602	0.5	624	0.6	0.1
White	81,632	88.4	100,227	88.1	99,502	87.9	−0.5
Other	1,336	1.4	1,551	1.4	71	0.1	N/A[b]
Total respondents	92,318	100.0	113,823	100.0	113,222	100.0	

Note: Sums on different tables may vary due to rounding and patterns of response.
[a]This is a new category for 1995.
[b]N/A means not applicable.

EDUCATION

The highest degree of the vast majority of NASW members is the MSW. Of the approximately 99 percent of members who responded to this question, 85.5 percent (129,824) held an MSW as their highest degree, down slightly from 87.8 percent in 1991 and 87.5 percent in 1988 (see Table 2.2).

In 1995, 9.9 percent (15,024) of responding members were BSW social workers, up from 7.4 percent in 1991 and 7.8 percent in 1988. Only 4.6 percent (6,994) of members reported holding a doctoral degree, relatively consistent with the 4.8 percent in 1991 and 4.7 percent in 1988.

The BLS occupational data for those occupying social work–titled positions show a broader range of educational background (see Figure 2.3). In 1994, BLS (1995) reported that 43.4 percent (289,000) of those in social work–titled positions had a bachelor's degree, 26.3 percent (175,000) had a master's degree, 12.7 percent (85,000) had some college but no degree, 8.7 percent (58,000) had a high school diploma, 6.8 percent (45,000) had an associate's degree, 1.2 percent (8,000) had a doctoral degree, and 0.8 percent (5,000) did not complete high school.

TABLE 2.2

Highest Degree Held by NASW Members

Highest Degree	1988 n	1988 %	1991 n	1991 %	1995 n	1995 %	Percentage Change 1988–1995
BSW	8,417	7.8	9,799	7.4	15,024	9.9	2.1
MSW	93,979	87.5	115,766	87.8	129,824	85.5	–2.0
PhD–DSW	5,058	4.7	6,359	4.8	6,994	4.6	–0.1
Total respondents	107,454	100	131,924	100	151,842	100	

FIGURE 2.3

Degrees Held by NASW Members Compared with BLS Respondents

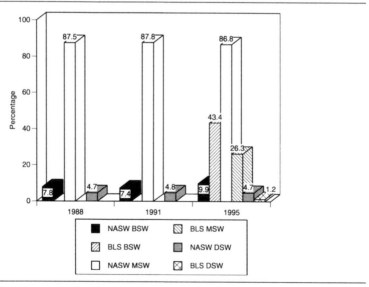

Note: BLS = Bureau of Labor Statistics.

23

Date of Highest Social Work Degree

Over half of responding NASW members, 52.5 percent (78,174), received their highest social work degree after 1985. Of the 148,917 members responding to this question, 30.1 percent (44,814) received their highest degree between 1990 and 1995. Consistent with earlier trends, there is a discernible pattern in the loss of members who received their highest social work degree in 1980 or earlier. For example, in 1988 the proportion of members with a degree date of 1980 or earlier was 66.9 percent, whereas in 1991 it was 46.8 percent (see Figure 2.4). By 1995, only 35.1 percent (52,123) of responding members indicated a degree date of 1980 or earlier. The proportion of members with a degree date between 1960 and 1970 dropped from 19.2 percent in 1988 to 12.4 percent in 1991 and to 9.1 percent in 1995. Overall, it appears that the membership is getting younger.

These data may reflect the socioeconomic environment of the times in that the enrollment in schools of social work declined during the late

FIGURE 2.4

Percentage of NASW Members, by Date of Highest Social Work Degree

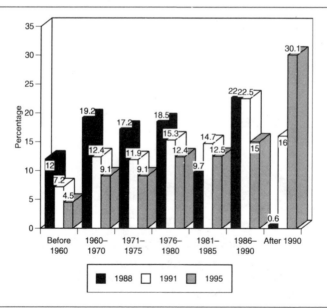

1970s and early 1980s (CSWE, 1986). These losses were somewhat compensated for by the increase in enrollments in the late 1980s, as reflected in the number of recent graduates who became NASW members in 1988 (2,792) and 1990 (4,628). Also, there seems to be a delay between the receipt of a degree and membership in NASW.

Nonetheless, the postdegree experience of NASW members is decreasing. In 1995, 79.1 percent of the responding members received their highest social work degree after 1970, compared with 80.4 percent in 1991 and 68.0 percent in 1988. By 1995, 57.6 percent (96,794) of the members earned their highest degree after 1980, up significantly from 53.2 percent of the members in 1991.

AGE

The median age range of NASW members in all three study years was 41 to 45 years. In the 1988 and 1991 study years, the median age of 41 to 45 years corresponded with national demographics on the baby-boom generation. However, by 1995, these baby boomers were approaching age 50, as reflected in the 17.3 percent (24,669) of responding members in the age 46 to 50 category. The fact that the median age of members has remained constant suggests that the membership is getting younger.

There is further evidence that the NASW membership is getting younger. In 1988, 8.5 percent of responding members were age 30 or under, compared with 14.6 percent of the members responding in 1991 and 16.2 percent in 1995. Members age 51 and over decreased in this period, from 28.8 percent of the members responding in 1988 to 23.4 percent in 1991 and 28.1 percent in 1995 (see Figure 2.5). Nevertheless, the single largest age category in 1995 was that of 51 to 60.

GEOGRAPHIC DISTRIBUTION OF MEMBERS

The geographic distribution of NASW members was compared with the standard regions of the United States used by the U.S. Department of Health and Human Services. The data indicate little change in geographic distribution for the three study years. The largest geographic distributions of members were in the Mid-Atlantic, East North Central, South Atlantic, and Pacific regions, the largest U.S. population centers. However, shifts from the North and Northeast to the South and Southwest, consistent with shifts in the general population, have also been characteristic since 1988 (see Table 2.3).

FIGURE 2.5

Percentage of NASW Members, by Age

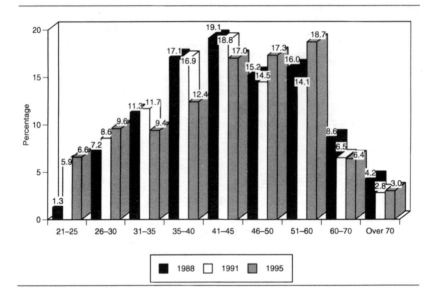

TABLE 2.3

Percentage of NASW Members, by Geographic Distribution

Region	1988	1991	1995	Percentage Change 1988–1995
East North Central	19.1	18.8	18.5	–0.6
East South Central	3.0	3.2	3.6	0.6
Mid-Atlantic	23.6	22.9	22.6	–1.0
Mountain	4.3	4.6	5.1	0.7
New England	10.5	10.4	10.1	–0.4
Pacific	12.4	12.2	11.6	–0.8
South Atlantic	14.0	14.7	15.3	1.3
Territories	0.1	0.1	0.3	0.2
West North Central	6.5	6.5	5.9	–0.6
West South Central	6.5	6.7	7.0	0.5
Total respondents	115,776	133,739	153,588	

EXPERIENCE

Approximately 64 percent (98,386) of the 153,814 members responded to the question about experience in 1995, down significantly from a 1991 response rate of 83 percent. In 1995 the two largest groups of respondents were those with six to 10 years of experience, at 18.8 percent (18,465), and those with 11 to 15 years of experience, at 18.5 percent (18,155) (see Figure 2.6).

Since 1988, the experience level of NASW members has steadily decreased. In 1995, 9.6 percent (9,421) of the 98,386 responding members had more than 25 years of experience, compared with 13.5 percent in 1991 and 21.4 percent in 1988.

The average years of experience reported by the 1995 respondents were six to 10 years, unchanged from 1991 and down from 11 to 15 years in 1988. These data, when combined with the data on the date of receipt of the highest degree and the age of the members, suggest a continuing and dramatic reversal in the pattern of experience of NASW members, from very experienced in 1988 to much less experienced in 1995.

FIGURE 2.6

Percentage of NASW Members, by Years of Work Experience

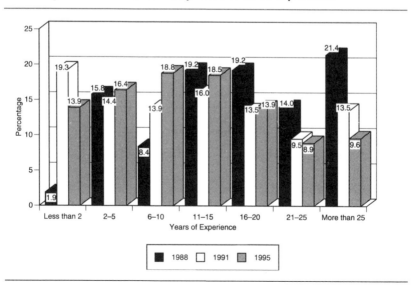

27

FIGURE 2.7

Percentage of NASW Members, by Years of Work Experience (Collapsed Categories)

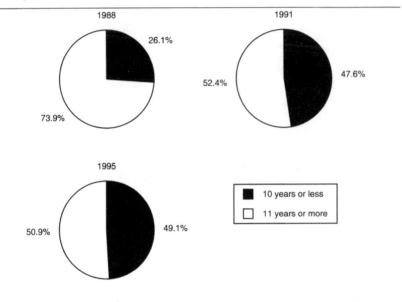

This reversal of the pattern is even more evident when the data are combined into two categories—zero to 10 years of experience and 11 or more years of experience (see Figure 2.7). In 1995, 49.1 percent (48,322) of respondents had zero to 10 years of experience, in contrast to 47.6 percent in 1991 and 26.1 percent in 1988. In 1995, 50.9 percent (50,064) had 11 or more years of experience, down from 52.4 percent in 1991 and 73.9 percent in 1988. These shifts are examined in greater detail in chapter 3.

Full-Time versus Part-Time Employment

Of the 61,864 members who responded to the question about full- or part-time employment in 1995, 76.5 percent (47,305) indicated that they were employed full-time and 23.5 percent (14,559) reported they were employed part-time. The proportion of members employed full-time has dropped slightly from 1991, when 77 percent of the members

FIGURE 2.8

Percentage of NASW Members, by Working Status

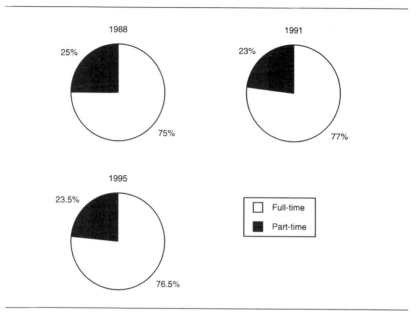

reported that they were employed full-time. Nevertheless, over the three study periods, the proportion of members working full- versus part-time has remained relatively steady (see Figure 2.8).

PRACTICE

Areas

In 1995 the top primary practice areas of the members were, in order, mental health, children and families, medical, and "other." This pattern is similar to that of 1991 and 1988. However, the new data collection form combines families and children, whereas the earlier form differentiated between family- and child-oriented practice. In both 1988 and 1991, the top primary practice areas of members were, in order, mental health, children, medical clinics, and family services (see Table 2.4). For purposes of comparison, 1991 and 1988 data for the separate categories of children and family services have been combined.

TABLE 2.4

Percentage of NASW Members, by Primary and Secondary Practice Areas

Area of Practice	1988		1991		1995	
	Primary	Secondary	Primary	Secondary	Primary	Secondary
Children's services[a]	17.0	12.0	17.3	12.6		
Combined[a]	5.2	6.7	5.8	6.6		
Community organization–planning[a]	1.6	2.8	1.2	2.2		
Corrections[a]	1.5	1.5	1.3	1.6		
Family services	12.2	20.6	11.4	19.1	25.5	29.0
Groups[a]	0.6	2.8	0.5	2.9		
Medical clinics	12.9	5.9	12.2	5.7	12.8	6.6
Mental health services	29.0	25.1	30.5	26.3	37.6	31.8
Occupational social work	0.8	1.0	0.8	0.9	0.8	1.0
Public assistance[a]	1.0	0.8	1.0	0.7		
School social work	4.2	2.2	4.4	2.5	5.1	2.7
Services to elderly people	5.3	6.3	5.1	5.4	4.9	5.5
Services to persons with mental retardation and developmental and physical disabilities[a]	3.7	3.7	3.6	3.6		
Substance abuse services[a]	4.1	7.6	4.7	9.7		
Other	0.9	1.0	0.2	0.2	12.0	21.8
Total respondents	89,443	35,666	107,921	44,441	100,556	42,554

[a]Categories were reconfigured for 1995. See appendix 2 for complete recoding.

Mental health continues to dominate the practice areas. In 1995, 37.6 percent (37,813) of members indicated that mental health was their primary practice area, up from 30.5 percent in 1991 and 29.0 percent in 1988.

In 1995, 27.6 percent (42,554) of the total data set of 153,814 indicated a secondary practice area, compared with 33.1 percent in 1991 and 30.7 percent in 1988. For the three study years, the vast majority of NASW members (over two-thirds) either did not have or failed to indicate that they had a secondary practice area.

The secondary practice areas were, in rank order and proportion, similar to those of the primary practice areas. In 1995, 31.8 percent (13,517) of respondents cited mental health as their secondary practice area, a significant increase over earlier years. In 1991, 26.3 percent of respondents and in 1988, 25.1 percent of respondents indicated that mental health was their secondary practice area. The second-ranked category of child–family services remained consistent for all three years. In 1995, 29.0 percent (12,346) of the respondents cited families and children as their secondary practice area, compared with 31.7 percent in 1991 and 32.6 percent in 1988.

Settings

The revised data collection form includes new primary setting categories, including managed care and business and industry. The category of mental health has also been broken down by inpatient or outpatient care. Nevertheless, in 1988, 1991, and 1995, the rankings (but not the proportion) of the top four primary practice settings cited by respondents were virtually identical (see Table 2.5). In 1995, 21.5 percent (21,386) of 99,564 respondents declared social services agencies to be their primary setting of practice, compared with 25.0 percent in 1991 and 26.0 percent in 1988. The second-, third-, and fourth-ranked settings were hospital, clinic, and private solo practice for 1988 and 1991 and health (inpatient), health (outpatient), and private solo practice for 1995.

The most significant proportional increase in setting of practice was in the area of private solo practice. For 1995, 14.0 percent (13,972) of respondents indicated private solo practice to be their primary setting of practice. In 1991, 10.9 percent of respondents and in 1988, 9.3 percent of respondents cited private solo practice as their primary setting.

Significant decreases were found in settings of health (inpatient) and social services agencies. Inpatient health as a setting (formerly "hospital") fell from 20.0 percent in 1991 and 19.9 percent in 1988 to 17.4

TABLE 2.5

Percentage of NASW Members, by Primary and Secondary Practice Settings

Setting	1988		1991		1995	
	Primary	Secondary	Primary	Secondary	Primary	Secondary
Agency	26.0	10.6	25.0	10.8	21.5	10.2
Business–industry[a]					0.2	0.1
Court	1.5	0.5	1.5	1.9	1.4	1.8
Group home[b]	2.7	3.3	3.1	3.4		
Health—inpatient[a]					17.4	7.3
Health—outpatient[a]					15.6	12.2
Hospital[b]	19.9	7.0	20.0	7.6		
Institution[b]	3.1	2.3	3.0	2.3		
Managed care[a]					0.2	0.2
Medical clinic[b]	16.2	12.6	16.2	12.9		
Membership organizations[b]	0.9	0.3	0.8	1.1		
Mental health—inpatient[a]					0.7	0.3
Mental health—outpatient[a]					2.4	1.7
Non–social work setting[b]	2.8	4.8	2.2	3.2		
Nursing home[b]	2.4	3.6	2.6	3.3		
Private group practice	3.8	11.3	4.1	11.6	4.9	11.7
Private solo practice	9.3	30.4	10.9	31.1	14.0	31.9
Residential facility[a]					7.1	7.6
School	5.8	2.5	5.9	2.9	6.6	2.9
University	4.2	8.2	4.6	8.1	4.5	8.0
Other[a]					3.4	4.0
Total respondents	87,247	27,555	106,194	32,676	99,564	32,370

[a]These are new categories for 1995.
[b]Categories were reconfigured for 1995. See appendix 2 for complete recoding.

percent (17,316) in 1995. This decline may be a reflection of widescale hospital downsizing experienced in recent years. Decreases in the proportion of NASW members with a primary setting of social services agencies may reflect the declassification of public social services, where a college degree in any area is the baseline educational requirement. In 1995, 21.5 percent (21,386) identified social services agencies as their primary work setting, compared with 25.0 percent in 1991 and 26.0 percent in 1988.

Similarly, the rank and proportion of the top four secondary practice settings for 1988, 1991, and 1995 were closely aligned. For the three study years, the rank order was private solo practice, outpatient health facility, private group practice, and social services agency. The proportion of NASW members citing private solo practice continued to increase slightly, at 31.9 percent (10,319 of 32,370 respondents to this question), up from 31.1 percent in 1991 and 30.4 percent in 1988. Other variations were negligible.

Colleges and universities ranked fifth among the secondary practice settings for the three years. In 1995, 8.0 percent (2,588) of the members who responded cited colleges and universities as their secondary practice setting, similar to 8.1 percent in 1991 and 8.2 percent in 1988. A larger proportion of NASW members who were affiliated with universities worked in these settings part-time rather than full-time.

Auspices

The four highest-ranked primary auspices under which NASW members worked remained consistent in the three study years, although there were some significant proportional shifts (see Table 2.6). In 1995 and 1991, private not-for-profit, private for-profit, public local, and public state auspices were most frequently cited. For 1988, local government ranked just slightly ahead of state government for third place.

There has been a consistent downward trend in the proportion of NASW members working in the public sector. Of the 97,884 members responding in 1995, 34.4 percent (33,611) noted that their primary auspice was public (federal, state, local, or military) compared with 38.7 percent in 1991 and 41.6 percent in 1988. This downward trend in public auspices was offset by the growth in the proportion of respondents who cited private for-profit as their primary auspice, from 18.5 percent in 1988, to 22.2 percent in 1991, to 27.1 percent (26,512) in 1995.

Of the 26,447 NASW members who indicated a secondary auspice in 1995, 48.7 percent (12,881) listed the private for-profit sector. This

TABLE 2.6

Percentage of NASW Members, by Primary and Secondary Auspice of Practice

Auspice	1988		1991		1995	
	Primary	Secondary	Primary	Secondary	Primary	Secondary
Private for-profit	18.5	45.4	22.2	46.5	27.1	48.7
Private not-for-profit[a]					38.6	29.9
Private not-for-profit nonsectarian[b]	28.1	20.8	26.7	20.6		
Private not-for-profit sectarian[b]	11.8	8.7	12.4	9.0		
Public federal	3.4	2.5	2.8	1.9	2.7	1.7
Public local	18.9	10.8	19.2	10.7	17.3	9.7
Public military	0.8	0.9	0.8	0.9	0.9	0.7
Public state	18.5	10.9	15.9	10.4	13.4	9.3
Total respondents	87,032	21,569	102,617	26,605	97,884	26,447

[a]This is a new category for 1995, which combines private not-for-profit sectarian and nonsectarian.
[b]Categories were collapsed to private not-for-profit.

sector has also experienced the largest proportional growth over the three time periods. In 1991, 46.5 percent of responding members indicated a secondary auspice of the for-profit sector, up from 45.4 in 1988. At the same time, the proportion of members indicating state or local government as their secondary auspice has decreased.

In all three study years, the second-ranked secondary auspice was the private not-for-profit sector, at 29.9 percent (7,902) in 1995, 29.6 percent in 1991, and 29.5 percent in 1988.

Functions of Members

In the three study years, responding members have overwhelmingly identified direct service as their primary function: 68.6 percent (70,620 of the 102,918 respondents) in 1995, 68.0 percent in 1991, and 64.1 percent in 1988. The second-ranked function in all three years was administration–management, at 15.3 percent (15,790) in 1995, 15.4 percent in 1991, and 16.8 percent in 1988. For 1995 and 1991, supervision ranked third, followed by teaching (see Table 2.7).

The rankings remained relatively stable for the three study years. Modest upward changes were noted for direct practice and a downward trend was seen in supervision. These data suggest a significant skewing between direct (micro) and indirect (macro) primary functions in social work practice. For 1995, the policy, community organization, and research functions combined represented only 1.8 percent (1,780) of respondents. (Note that in the 1994 revised demographic form, planning and consultation were dropped as categories and community organization was added.) When management was factored in, the total for macro practice was 17.1 percent (17,570), down from 18.4 percent in 1991 and 20.1 percent in 1988.

A sizable proportion of the members reported that they performed multiple functions in one or more settings. Of the full data set of 153,814 in 1995, 31.4 percent (48,346) reported a secondary function, down from 38 percent in 1991. Direct service, the largest category, represented 35.2 percent (17,028) of these respondents.

The proportions and rankings of secondary functions were consistent for the three study years. For 1995 and 1991, supervision, teaching, and "other" were ranked third, fourth, and fifth. For 1988, those rankings, in order, were supervision, "other," and teaching. Supervision appears to be carried out by social workers significantly more frequently as a secondary rather than primary function. And the high proportion of

TABLE 2.7

Percentage of NASW Members, by Primary and Secondary Functions

Function	1988		1991		1995	
	Primary	Secondary	Primary	Secondary	Primary	Secondary
Community organization–advocacy[a]					0.3	0.3
Consultant[b]	1.8	14.0	1.5	14.0		
Direct service	64.1	32.6	68.0	32.1	68.6	35.2
Education[b]	5.0	15.5	4.5	15.7		
Management	16.8	10.2	15.4	10.2	15.3	9.9
Non–social work[b]	4.5	3.3	2.7	2.1		
Planning[b]	0.5	2.6	0.4	2.4		
Policy	0.5	2.5	0.5	2.4	0.9	4.0
Research	0.5	2.2	0.6	2.2	0.6	2.1
Supervision	6.2	17.2	6.2	18.9	5.5	18.1
Teaching[a]					4.6	15.4
Training[a]					0.1	0.2
Other[a]					4.1	14.8
Total respondents	94,822	42,244	110,349	51,418	102,918	48,346

[a]These are new categories for 1995. Teaching relates to formal social work education; training relates to agency-based training programs.
[b]Categories were reconfigured for 1995. See appendix 2 for complete recoding.

Demographic Overview

TABLE 2.8

Percentage of NASW Members, by Primary and Secondary Focus of Work, 1995[a]

Focus	Primary	Secondary
Alcohol–drugs	9.6	9.1
Disabilities	6.0	3.4
Employment-related	1.7	1.7
Family issues	26.7	26.5
Grief–bereavement	2.5	5.9
Health	14.6	8.1
Housing	0.7	0.7
Income maintenance	0.5	0.5
Individual–behavior	22.2	28.2
International	0.2	0.6
Violence–victims assistance	2.3	3.5
Other	13.0	11.9
Total respondents	14,194	4,521

[a]Note: This is a new category for 1995. No previous data are available.

social workers with a secondary function of teaching is consistent with findings regarding secondary practice settings.

Primary Focus

In the revised demographic form, a question was added regarding the primary focus of members' work (see Table 2.8). Family issues were ranked first as the primary focus of the 14,194 responding members, at 26.7 percent (3,793). The second-ranked primary focus was individual–behavior at 22.2 percent (3,158) followed by health at 14.6 percent (2,077). Least frequently cited were employment-related, housing, income maintenance, and international issues. However, the small response rate (about 9 percent of the total data set) may skew these findings.

The revised demographic profile form also requested information about a secondary focus, if any. Here, only 4,521 (2.9 percent) of members responded. Individual–behavior ranked first at 28.2 percent (1,274), followed by family issues at 26.5 percent (1,198).

Clients Seen

Another new question on the revised demographic form concerned the number of clients seen by social workers per year. This question may have misled some respondents, who may have different understandings of the time period (that is, caseload size at any given time) or the definition of "client" (that is, family or group). The confusing nature of this question may account for the poor response rate of about 7 percent (11,447). Of those responding, 45.8 percent (5,238) indicated that they see between 1 and 100 clients, and 20.8 percent (2,385) see between 101 and 200 clients. Approximately 14 percent (1,612) of responding members indicated that they see from 500 to more than 900 clients.

ACSW STATUS

The percentage of NASW members holding active ASCW status continues to fall (see Figure 2.9). In 1995, 37.6 percent of the members reported having active ACSW status, compared with 45.2 percent in 1991 and 50.6 percent (58,987) in 1988. This significant decrease may be attributed, in part, to members opting for state licensure as their primary credential.

LICENSING

The new membership application–renewal demographic form introduced in 1994 included, for the first time, a question about whether members hold a practice license. Although only 10.1 percent (15,540) of the total 1995 membership responded to this question, the vast majority of respondents, 80.7 percent (12,540), indicated that they hold a practice license.

PUBLIC OFFICE

Members were also asked for the first time in 1994 whether they have held public office. Of the 15,492 members who responded to this question, 1.4 percent (219) indicated that they hold public office. Only 199 social workers were identified by the NASW Political Affairs Office in 1995 as serving in elective office (NASW, 1995). A content analysis of the titles of the offices held indicated that members interpreted this survey question to mean both elected and appointed office; this difference in interpretation may explain the difference in numbers.

FIGURE 2.9

Percentage of NASW Members, by ACSW Status

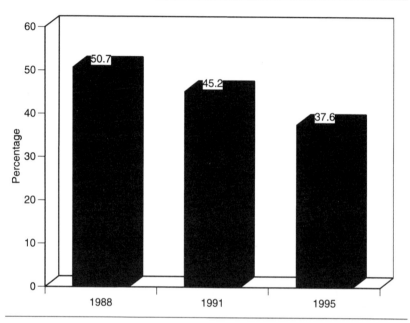

Note: ACSW = Academy of Certified Social Workers.

MEMBERSHIP CATEGORY

In 1995, as in 1988 and 1991, the vast majority of respondents were full members (see Table 2.9). However, the proportion of full members to other categories of membership has steadily decreased. In 1995, 62.5 percent of respondents held full membership, compared with 64.9 percent in 1991 and 65.1 percent in 1988. At the same time, the proportion of student members has grown. In 1995, 15 percent of the membership was composed of students at the PhD–DSW, MSW, or BSW levels; most of the students were studying for their MSWs. In both 1991 and 1988, 12.8 percent of the membership was composed of students.

The transitional category comprised 11.1 percent (17,135) of the membership in 1995, up from 10.2 percent in 1991 and 9.0 percent in 1988. This category includes social workers who completed their

TABLE 2.9

Percentage of NASW Members, by Category of Membership

Category	1988	1991	1995
BSW	1.6	2.2	1.9
Foreign	0.9	0.4	0.3
MSW	61.0	60.3	58.3
PhD–DSW	2.5	2.4	2.3
Retired	3.0	2.7	2.5
Student BSW	3.0	3.4	4.6
Student MSW	9.0	8.5	9.5
Student PhD–DSW	0.8	0.9	0.9
Transitional BSW	1.5	2.1	2.4
Transitional MSW	7.5	8.1	8.7
Other	9.2	9.0	8.6
Total respondents	116,296	134,240	153,814

highest degree within the past two years and were transferring from BSW or MSW student status to full-member status (and therefore received a discount on the full-membership dues). The growth in the proportion of student and transitional members to full-time members suggests that the membership is becoming less experienced.

CHAPTER HIGHLIGHTS

- The vast majority of NASW members were women, and the ratio of women to men increased.
- The vast majority of members were white.
- The overwhelming majority of members had MSW degrees.
- Approximately 86.4 percent of the 1995 members received their highest social work degree after 1971, a significant increase over 1988 and 1991.
- In 1995, almost 40 percent of the members had 10 years or less of social work experience, a sharp contrast with 1988, when the largest proportion had more than 26 years of experience.
- The median age of the members for 1988, 1991, and 1995 was 41 to 45 years.
- Findings on the date of receipt of the highest social work degree and years of experience indicated that the membership is getting younger.

- More than 75 percent of the members were employed full-time.
- Mental health services continued to represent the largest primary practice area in 1995, followed by children and families, medical, and "other."
- Approximately 28 percent of members indicated a secondary practice area in 1995, a decrease from 1991 and 1988.
- Mental health services represented the largest secondary practice area in all three years.
- The four highest-ranked primary practice settings in 1995 were social services agencies, health (inpatient), health (outpatient), and private solo practice.
- Private solo practice ranked first as the secondary practice setting in all three years. The proportion of members in private solo practice as a secondary setting is increased.
- Private not-for-profit, private for-profit, public local, and public state were the highest-ranked primary auspices in 1995.
- The number and proportion of members employed under public auspices decreased.
- The number and proportion of members employed under private for-profit auspices increased.
- Relatively few members worked under federal auspices.
- Direct service was the primary function of the vast majority of members.
- The most frequently reported secondary function was also direct services.
- The primary focus of work for the largest proportion of members was family issues, followed by individual–behavior and health.
- The vast majority of respondents held a practice license. At the same time, however, the percentage of respondents holding active ASCW status continued to decrease.
- The largest percentage of members worked in the Mid-Atlantic region.

REFERENCES

Bureau of Labor Statistics. (1995, January). *Employment and earnings.* Washington, DC: Author.

Council on Social Work Education. (1986). *Statistics on social work education in the United States: 1985.* Washington, DC: Author.

National Association of Social Workers. (1995). *Social workers serving in elective offices.* Washington, DC: Author.

CHAPTER 3

WHO WE ARE

EMPLOYMENT STATUS, GENDER, AGE, ETHNICITY, EDUCATION,
GEOGRAPHIC REPRESENTATION, AND EXPERIENCE

—

This chapter presents findings on the demographics of a subset of
NASW members: those who were employed full- or part-time in 1995.
Thus, student, associate, and retired–unemployed members were
excluded from the analysis. For 1995, the total population of employed
social workers was 113,352. As applicable, comparisons are made with
1991 and 1988 member demographics to identify discernible trends
over time. It should be recalled that when they complete the demographic profile each year as part of their membership renewal, many
members do not respond to all questions. Thus, the number of responses may vary considerably from question to question.

FULL- VERSUS PART-TIME EMPLOYMENT STATUS

The part-time social work labor force is growing. Of the 48.3 percent
(54,799) employed NASW members who responded to the question
about full- versus part-time employment in 1995, 22.2 percent (12,189)
indicated that they were employed part-time (see Figure 3.1). In 1991,
21.2 percent of responding members indicated that they worked part-
time, up from 18.6 percent in 1988. (Note that on the membership
application form, the question about full- versus part-time employment
status is listed as a subcategory of the question about current annual
salary from primary employment only; it is within the context of this
question that the respondents were asked to indicate whether their
annual salary is for full- or part-time employment.)

There is a much higher proportion of women than men employed
part-time. Of members employed part-time in 1995, 91.6 percent were

FIGURE 3.1

Percentage of Working NASW Members, by Full-Time versus Part-Time
Employment Status

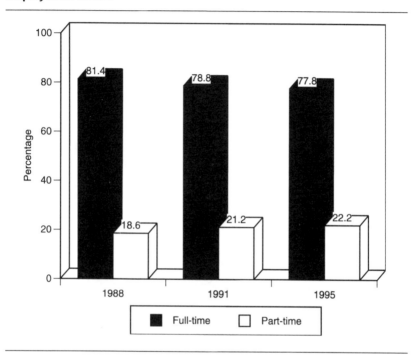

women, whereas only 78.3 percent of all employed NASW members
were women. A higher proportion of younger NASW members are
employed part-time than older members; of members between the ages
of 21 and 25, 52.9 percent were employed part-time. This age group
may represent those enrolled in part-time MSW programs or those
entering the job market for the first time. White members are overrepresented among the part-time social work labor force; 23.4 percent of
responding white members identified their employment status as part-
time, slightly above the 22.2 percent for all employed members. Those
members at the BSW level are also substantially more likely to be
employed part-time than are members with the MSW or PhD–DSW as
their highest degree. In 1995, 30.9 percent of responding BSW members
indicated that they were employed part-time.

GENDER

Of the 113,352 employed NASW members in 1995, 98.3 percent (111,464) responded to the question about gender. In that year, 78.3 percent (87,331) were women. As indicated in Figure 3.2, the proportion of women within the NASW membership continues to grow. In 1991, 75.7 percent of responding employed members were women, up from 72.3 percent in 1988.

Gender, by Highest Social Work Degree

The proportion of female to male NASW members varies according to highest degree held (see Figure 3.3). Although 78.3 percent of all employed members in 1995 were women, 89.7 percent of members with a BSW as their highest degree were women, compared with 78.5

FIGURE 3.2

Percentage of Working NASW Members, by Gender

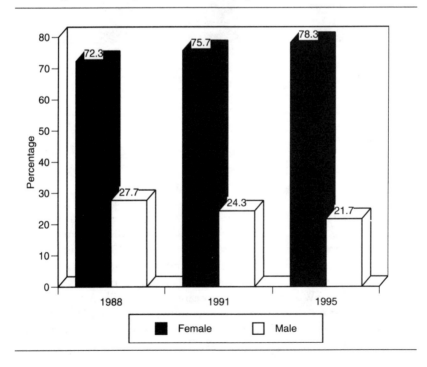

FIGURE 3.3

Percentage of Working NASW Members, by Gender and Highest Degree, 1995

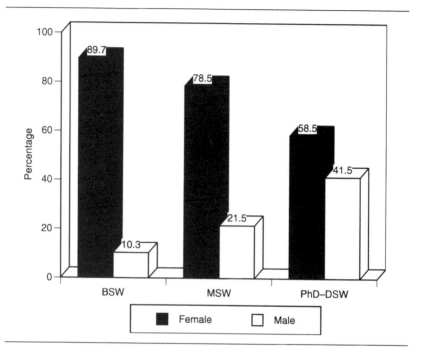

percent with an MSW and 58.5 percent with a PhD–DSW. The composition of the NASW membership is becoming more female, although women have constituted the majority of members since the association's inception (Becker, 1961). The proportion of women rose steadily between 1988 and 1995 in each degree category.

Gender, by Date of Highest Social Work Degree

The feminization of the membership is highlighted when gender is examined in relation to the date of receipt of the highest social work degree. For example, in the 1995 data set, 36.6 percent of members who received their highest degree between 1961 and 1970 were men. Furthermore, men constituted 30.0 percent or more of the membership who received their highest degree between 1931 and 1976, with the notable exception of the period 1941 to 1950. The decrease in the proportion of male members receiving their degrees in those years should be viewed within the context of World War II and the proportion of all U.S. men then serving in the military (see Figure 3.4).

In sharp contrast are findings for 1986 to 1990, when 16.9 percent of those who obtained their highest degree were men. For those who received their degree between 1990 and 1995, the proportion of men dropped to 14.8 percent. The downward trend in the ratio of male to female members has been consistent since 1961.

Gender, by Ethnicity

Although the majority of members in all ethnic groups were women in all three years, there are some proportional differences among the male members by ethnicity. Proportionately, there were fewer African American male NASW members than male NASW members of other ethnic

FIGURE 3.4

Percentage of Working NASW Members, by Gender and Date of Highest Degree, 1995

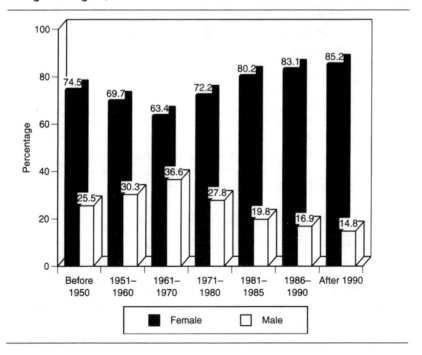

groups, at 19.0 percent in 1995, 19.4 percent in 1991, and 22.2 percent in 1988. In contrast, there were proportionately more Chicano male members than male members of other ethnic groups, at 33.6 percent in 1995, 36.3 percent in 1991, and 39.2 percent in 1988 (see Table 3.1).

Gender, by Age

The feminization of the NASW membership is further discernible when gender is examined in relation to age. The proportion of women to men increases for younger NASW members. In 1995, for example, 94.2 percent of respondents between the ages of 21 and 25 were women, as were 89.6 percent of those between the ages of 26 and 30. The ratio of women to men more closely approximates that of the overall membership among NASW members age 41 or older (see Table 3.2).

In 1995, 76 percent of responding male members were age 41 or older. This finding is consistent with findings that related gender to the date of the highest social work degree. In that same year, the percentage of female members age 41 and older was 63.1. Thus, the proportion of female members was much higher in the younger age groups and the proportion of male members was higher in the older age groups.

TABLE 3.1

Percentage of Working NASW Members, by Gender and Ethnicity

	1988		1991		1995	
Ethnicity	Female	Male	Female	Male	Female	Male
African American	77.8	22.2	80.6	19.4	81.0	19.0
American Indian	70.3	29.7	76.6	23.4	78.2	21.8
Asian	70.9	29.1	72.8	27.2	76.4	23.6
Chicano	60.8	39.2	63.7	36.3	66.4	33.6
Mixed heritage[a]					71.3	28.7
Other Hispanic	74.6	25.4	77.7	22.3	77.9	22.1
Puerto Rican	74.5	25.5	77.4	22.6	75.3	24.7
White	73.2	26.8	76.3	23.7	77.7	22.3
Other	73.2	26.8	68.4	31.6	63.0	37.0
Total respondents	45,844	16,778	64,218	20,003	71,903	20,652

Note: All percentages are rounded to the nearest tenth. For 1988 and 1991, figures are the percentage responding to both gender and ethnicity questions.
[a]This is a new category for 1995.

TABLE 3.2

NASW Members, by Age and Gender, 1995

	Female		Male		Total Respondents	
Age in Years	n	%	n	%	n	%
Under 21	15	78.9	4	21.1	19	—
21–25	3,318	94.2	205	5.8	3,523	3.4
26–30	7,683	89.6	896	10.4	8,579	8.2
31–35	8,349	84.1	1,582	15.9	9,931	9.5
36–40	10,897	80.1	2,706	19.9	13,603	13.0
41–45	14,955	75.2	4,943	24.8	19,898	19.0
46–50	15,635	74.8	5,261	25.2	20,896	20.0
51–60	17,325	75.4	5,662	24.6	22,987	22.0
61–70	3,691	75.9	1,171	24.1	4,862	4.6
over 70	251	83.1	51	16.9	302	0.3
Total	82,119	78.5	22,481	21.5	104,600	100.0

Note: Dash means percentage is so small as to be statistically insignificant.

Also in 1995, women made up 75 percent or more of most age categories, consistent with their proportion in the overall membership. However, there were exceptions at both ends of the age continuum. In the over-70 category, 83.1 percent of the members were women, perhaps because of the longer life span of American women. In the 21- to 25-year-old category, 94.2 percent of respondents were women, whereas 89.6 percent of those age 26 to 30 were women. The large proportion of women at the younger end of the spectrum again suggests the increasing feminization of the profession.

AGE

Shifts in the age of NASW members offer an inconsistent picture. The median age of employed NASW members in all three study years was 41 to 45. However, in 1995, 42.0 percent (44,344 of the 105,587 employed members who responded to this question) were between the ages of 46 and 60, up from 33.0 percent for this age group in 1991 and 35.7 percent in 1988. This increase may represent the aging of the baby boom generation, but proportional changes in the age of employed NASW members over the three study years are not readily explainable.

In 1995, 34.0 percent (35,954) of the members who responded were 40 or younger, down significantly from 41.6 percent in 1991 but more consistent with 35.0 percent in 1988. The year 1991 may signify an anomaly in the data rather than a shift in demographics (see Figure 3.5).

As expected, members whose highest degree is the BSW tend to be younger than the other NASW members. In 1995, 48.1 percent of BSW members who responded were age 21 to 30, up significantly from 38.3 percent in 1991 and 27.0 percent in 1988 (see Table 3.3).

The majority of respondents holding doctoral degrees continued to fall within the age range of 41 to 60. In 1995, 81.3 percent (3,326) of the 105,065 members responding to questions about both degree and age were between the ages of 41 and 60.

FIGURE 3.5

Percentage of Working NASW Members, by Age

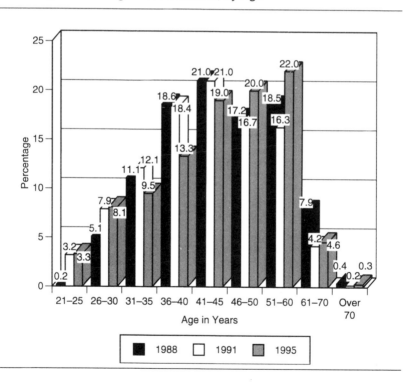

TABLE 3.3

Percentage of Working NASW Members, by Age and Highest Social Work Degree

Age in Years	BSW			MSW			PhD–DSW		
	1988	1991	1995	1988	1991	1995	1988	1991	1995
21–30	27.0	38.3	48.1	3.7	10.0	9.6	0.5	1.0	0.6
31–40	29.5	28.5	21.3	30.3	31.3	23.2	9.5	13.9	8.3
41–50	22.1	21.2	20.0	39.3	38.3	40.2	45.0	47.6	42.3
51–60	14.7	9.6	8.9	18.6	16.2	22.1	28.0	28.3	39.0
Over 60	6.8	2.3	1.6	8.2	4.3	5.0	17.0	9.3	9.8
Total respondents	3,696	4,911	6,303	66,342	82,633	94,672	2,970	3,750	4,090
Percent of total	5.1	5.4	6.0	90.9	90.5	90.1	4.1	4.1	3.9

Age, by Date of Highest Social Work Degree

In 1995, 65.2 percent (66,236 of 101,657 respondents) of responding members had obtained their highest degree after 1981. The largest proportional increase over the three study years occurred in the 1990–1995 category. In 1995, 30.0 percent of responding members indicated that they had obtained their highest degree after 1990, suggesting the relative youth of the NASW membership.

As expected, there is a high correlation between the age of members and the year they obtained their highest social work degree. However, as Table 3.4 shows, in 1995 a significant number of members were in the category of "nontraditional" students who did not go directly from undergraduate to graduate education and thus were older than other graduate students when they completed their social work education. For example, 29.2 percent (6,524) of those age 51 to 60 received their highest social work degree in the 1980s, when they were 37 to 46 years old. Similarly, 14.2 percent (2,882) of those age 46 to 50 received their highest social work degree between 1981 and 1985, again when they were over 30 years old. Age in relation to the date of receipt of the highest social work degree may reflect career changes after several years of work experience or the fulfillment of family obligations before the pursuit of professional education.

It is interesting to note that the closest association between age and the date of receipt of the highest social work degree was found for respondents age 21 to 25 and 26 to 30. In 1995, 96.9 percent (3,517) of members between the ages of 21 and 25 and 84.5 percent (7,299) of those between 26 and 30 earned their highest social work degree after 1990. In contrast, of those age 41 to 50, 84.6 percent (16,699) earned their degrees between 1971 and 1980. And of those age 51 to 60, 27.0 percent (6,032) earned their degrees between 1961 and 1970.

ETHNICITY

The ethnic composition of employed NASW membership has remained relatively stable. The membership continues to be overwhelmingly white—88.5 percent in all three study years. Approximately 81.9 percent (92,814) of the 1995 data set of 113,352 employed members responded to the question about ethnicity (see Figure 3.6).

The proportion of people of color remained basically unchanged from 1988 to 1995. African Americans represented 5.3 percent (4,904) of the respondents in 1995, down slightly from 5.6 percent in both

TABLE 3.4

Percentage of Working NASW Members, by Age and Date of Highest Social Work Degree, 1995

Age in Years	Date of Highest Social Work Degree							Total Respondents
	Before 1950	1951– 1960	1961– 1970	1971– 1980	1981– 1985	1986– 1990	After 1990	
21–25	—	—	0.1	1.0	—	0.1	96.9	3,545
26–30	—	—	—	—	0.1	14.8	84.5	8,582
31–35	—	—	0.1	0.2	11.0	44.6	43.7	9,798
36–40	—	—	0.2	10.6	33.1	27.3	28.2	13,005
41–45	—	0.1	0.2	40.6	19.7	17.7	21.6	19,101
46–50	—	0.1	5.2	44.0	14.2	16.7	19.5	20,329
51–60	0.1	1.4	27.0	28.1	13.7	15.5	13.9	22,308
Over 60	1.1	15.2	20.3	32.8	14.5	10.7	5.2	4,989
Total respondents	96	1,123	8,177	26,025	15,809	19,956	30,056	101,657
Percent of total	0.1	1.1	8.0	32.2	15.6	19.6	29.6	100.0

Note: Dash means percentage is so small as to be statistically insignificant.

FIGURE 3.6

Percentage of Working NASW Members, by Ethnicity

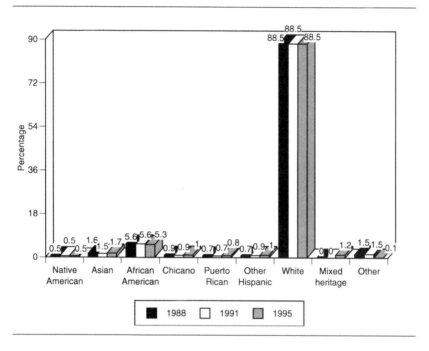

1988 and 1991. Hispanics, including Chicanos, Puerto Ricans, and Other Hispanics, constituted 2.8 percent (2,553) of the respondents in 1995, up from 2.3 percent in 1988 and 2.5 percent in 1991. Asians represented 1.7 percent (1,608) of the respondents in 1995, up slightly from 1.6 percent in 1988 and 1.5 percent in 1991.

Ethnicity, by Gender

An examination of ethnicity in relation to gender reveals a consistent trend with the overall NASW employed member profile. There are, however, some small variations. Eighty-one percent of employed African American members are women, compared with 77.7 percent of the employed members of all other ethnic groups. The proportion of African American women also increased between 1988 and 1995. In 1988, 77.8 percent of the African American respondents were women compared with 80.6 percent in 1991. However, the proportion of female Chicano members is lower than that in the employed membership as a whole. In 1995, 66.4 percent of Chicano members were women, up from 60.8 percent in 1988 and 63.7 percent in 1991. Recall that the proportion of women to men in the overall membership has grown consistently over the years.

Ethnicity, by Degree

Approximately 82 percent (92,353) of employed NASW members responded to the questions about ethnicity and degree in 1995. Native American and Chicano members are overrepresented at the BSW level, whereas Asian members and members of mixed heritage are overrepresented at the PhD–DSW level (see Table 3.5).

Ethnicity, by Date of Highest Social Work Degree

Several notable trends emerge when ethnicity is examined in relation to the date of receipt of the highest social work degree. Although still a small proportion of the total membership, the proportion of Other

TABLE 3.5

Percentage of Working NASW Members, by Ethnicity and Highest Degree, 1995

Ethnicity	BSW	MSW	PhD–DSW	Total Respondents
African American	4.8	89.3	5.9	4,868
Asian	2.7	90.1	7.1	1,603
Chicano	8.1	88.4	3.4	908
Mixed heritage	2.3	90.3	7.4	1,087
Native American	9.5	85.5	5.0	482
Other Hispanic	3.7	91.1	5.2	911
Puerto Rican	3.2	90.8	6.0	716
White	4.0	91.8	4.2	81,724
Other	5.6	92.6	1.9	54
Total respondents	3,787	84,540	4,026	92,353
Percent of total	4.1	91.5	4.4	100.0

Hispanic members has increased steadily since 1971. For example, of those who earned their highest degree before 1970, 2.1 percent (56 members) identified themselves as Other Hispanic, compared with 4.4 percent (362) of those who earned their highest degree after 1970. There has also been an upward trend in the proportion of Chicano and Puerto Rican members (see Table 3.6).

The proportion of African American NASW members with an early degree date has increased. Of members who earned their highest degree between 1971 and 1980, 6.0 percent (1,525) were African American compared with 8.7 percent (1,409) who did so between 1981 and 1990.

Overall, NASW does not seem to be attracting ethnic minority graduates in the same proportion as it is white graduates, reversing earlier trends. CSWE (Lennon, 1995) reported that 19.2 percent (2,468) of students awarded their MSW degree in 1994 were members of ethnic groups. This percentage is up considerably from earlier CSWE reports. Spaulding (1991) reported that from 1986 to 1991, 13.9 percent to 18.5 percent of social work degrees were earned by members of ethnic groups. The 1995 CSWE data suggest that NASW, with an ethnic group percentage of 11.5 in 1995, is lagging in its recruitment of recent MSW graduates of color.

Ethnicity, by Experience

Although the proportion of African American NASW members has remained static, experience levels suggest a potential decrease in the near future. In 1995, 56.9 percent (2,284) of African American respondents indicated that they had more than 10 years of experience compared with 43.1 percent (1,732) of African Americans with less than 10 years of experience. That same year, 49.4 percent of all working NASW members reported having less than 10 years of experience (see Table 3.7). Findings are similar for those of Asian heritage. Of those who identified their ethnicity as Asian, 56.1 percent (782) had 10 or more years of experience compared with 43.9 percent with less than 10 years of experience.

In contrast, the proportion of Native Americans, Chicanos, and Other Hispanics joining the profession and NASW has increased in recent years. The level of experience of these three groups was concentrated in the under-10-years category in 1995. For example, the highest proportion of Other Hispanic members had six to 10 years of experience, whereas the highest proportions of African American and Asian members had more than 16 years of experience.

TABLE 3.6

Percentage of Working NASW Members, by Ethnicity and Date of Highest Social Work Degree, 1995

Ethnicity	Date of Highest Social Work Degree							Total Respondents	Percentage Ethnicity
	Before 1950	1951– 1960	1961– 1970	1971– 1980	1981– 1985	1986– 1990	After 1990		
African American	7.3	9.2	5.2	6.0	4.5	4.2	5.8	4,754	5.3
Asian	0.8	2.9	2.2	1.9	1.5	1.6	1.6	1,551	1.7
Chicano	0.0	0.2	0.4	1.0	1.2	0.8	1.2	886	0.9
Mixed heritage	3.3	1.2	0.9	1.4	1.1	0.9	1.3	1,050	1.2
Native American	0.0	0.4	0.4	0.4	0.5	0.5	0.7	476	—
Other Hispanic	1.6	0.2	0.3	0.6	1.1	1.2	1.5	887	1.7
Puerto Rican	0.0	0.4	0.5	0.7	1.0	0.7	0.9	684	0.8
White	87.0	85.5	90.0	87.8	89.1	90.0	86.9	78,985	88.4
Other	0.0	0.1	0.1	0.1	0.1	0.0	0.1	52	—
Total respondents	123	1,220	8,497	25,331	14,106	18,574	21,241	89,325	
Percent of total	0.1	1.4	9.5	28.3	15.8	20.8	24.1		100.0

Note: Dash means percentage is so small as to be statistically insignificant.

TABLE 3.7

Percentage of Working NASW Members, by Ethnicity and Years of Experience, 1995

Ethnicity	Less than 2	2–5	6–10	11–15	16–20	21–25	More than 25	Total Respondents	Percentage Ethnicity
				Experience in Years					
African American	11.4	15.0	16.7	18.5	17.9	12.1	8.4	4,016	5.3
Asian	11.5	14.3	18.1	16.3	16.2	12.5	11.0	1,396	1.7
Chicano	15.7	16.7	21.5	21.8	14.5	7.4	2.4	785	1.0
Mixed heritage	12.7	14.9	18.7	21.7	16.5	8.9	6.6	884	1.2
Native American	15.1	19.6	18.4	16.7	17.5	7.2	5.5	418	0.5
Other Hispanic	19.9	21.5	24.3	16.9	9.3	4.7	3.4	794	1.0
Puerto Rican	11.1	16.3	23.1	23.1	15.3	5.8	5.3	640	0.8
White	13.8	16.8	19.0	19.6	14.7	9.1	7.1	70,237	88.4
Other	11.3	20.8	7.5	24.5	9.4	9.4	17.0	53	0.1
Total respondents	10,832	13,203	15,013	15,499	11,790	7,267	5,619	79,223	
Percent of total	13.7	16.7	19.0	19.6	14.9	9.2	7.1		100.0

EDUCATION

The vast majority of the employed NASW members who responded to this question in 1995—90.1 percent (101,360 of 112,518)—had an MSW as their highest degree (see Figure 3.7). The proportion of members at the MSW level has remained relatively constant: 90.5 percent in 1988 and 90.4 percent in 1991. The proportion of members at the doctoral level has also remained stable: 4.1 percent in 1995 and 4.3 percent in both 1988 and 1991.

In light of the proliferation of BSW programs in the past two decades, the absolute and proportional representation of BSWs in the NASW membership is surprisingly low. In 1995, there was a small gain in BSW membership, at 5.8 percent (6,562), up from 5.2 percent (5,213) in 1991 and 5.3 percent (4,252) in 1988. In 1994 alone, 10,511

FIGURE 3.7

Percentage of Working NASW Members, by Highest Degree

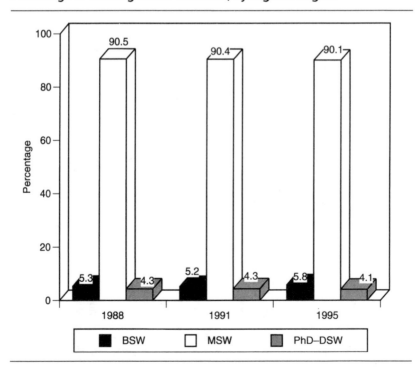

BSW degrees were awarded (Lennon, 1995) by 349 of 382 accredited BSW programs in the United States. NASW is not attracting members of this group.

Highest Degree, by Gender

Proportionately more men than women obtain doctoral degrees in social work (see Table 3.8). However, there has been a small but steady increase in the proportion of women who obtain doctorates. Of the members who had a PhD or DSW in 1995, 58.5 percent (2,625) were women and 41.5 percent (1,860) were men. In 1991, 55.0 percent of members with PhD–DSWs were women compared with 52.0 percent in 1988. The fact remains, however, that the number of men with PhDs or DSWs continues to be disproportionate to their overall representation in the membership.

The proportion of male members whose highest degree was the BSW also deviated from the proportion of men in the overall membership, but in the opposite direction. Of those whose highest degree was the BSW, 10.3 percent (671) were men, a significant decrease from 1991 (12.3 percent) and 1988 (17.5 percent).

Date of Highest Social Work Degree

Because many social work students enter graduate school as part of a career change or to start a career after raising a family, the date of receipt of the highest social work degree is a more accurate demographic variable than age when profiling the NASW members. This variable provides information about when members entered the professional social work labor force (see Table 3.9).

TABLE 3.8

Percentage of Working NASW Members, by Highest Degree and Gender, 1995

Year	BSW Female	BSW Male	MSW Female	MSW Male	PhD–DSW Female	PhD–DSW Male
1988	82.5	17.5	72.3	27.7	52.0	48.0
1991	87.7	12.3	75.9	24.1	55.0	45.0
1995	89.7	10.3	78.5	21.5	58.5	41.5

TABLE 3.9

Percentage of Working NASW Members, by Date of Highest
Social Work Degree

Date of Degree	1988	1991	1995
Before 1951	1.7	0.5	0.2
1951–1960	7.0	3.2	1.4
1961–1970	22.1	12.9	9.1
1971–1975	21.7	14.0	10.9
1976–1980	23.8	18.7	15.2
1981–1985	11.6	17.9	15.5
1986–1990	12.0	27.5	19.0
After 1990	0.1	5.4	28.7
Total respondents	59,137	92,013	109,009

In 1988, the period in which the largest proportion of members obtained their highest degrees was 1976 to 1980, whereas in 1991 and 1995 it was 1986 to 1990. In the 1995 data set, 49.7 percent (54,244 of 109,009 respondents) received their highest social work degree between 1976 and 1990 compared with 64.1 percent in 1991 and 47.4 percent in 1988. Again, we see a possible anomaly in the 1991 data. However, in 1995 the largest proportion of members, 28.7 percent, received their highest social work degree between 1990 and 1995. These findings suggest that since 1991 a significant proportion of the members joined NASW soon after they received their highest degree but that they may not remain members for many years.

GEOGRAPHIC DISTRIBUTION OF MEMBERS

Distribution of working NASW members has not changed dramatically between 1988 and 1995. However, the continued migration of social workers from the Rust Belt to the Sun Belt is apparent. The highest proportion of the 113,186 employed respondents, 22.8 percent (25,836), resided in the Mid-Atlantic states in 1995 compared with 23.2 percent in 1991 and 24.2 percent (20,738) in 1988 (see Tables 3.10 and 3.11). The second-ranked region of NASW membership was the East North Central region, where 18.5 percent (20,986) resided in 1995 compared with 18.8 percent in 1991 and 19.3 percent in 1988.

TABLE 3.10

States by Region

New England	East North Central	West South Central
Connecticut	Illinois	Arkansas
Maine	Indiana	Louisiana
Massachusetts	Michigan	Oklahoma
New Hampshire	Ohio	Texas
Rhode Island	Wisconsin	**Mountain**
Vermont	**West North Central**	Arizona
Mid-Atlantic	Iowa	Colorado
New Jersey	Kansas	Idaho
New York	Minnesota	Montana
Pennsylvania	Missouri	Nevada
South Atlantic	Nebraska	New Mexico
Delaware	North Dakota	Utah
District of Columbia	South Dakota	Wyoming
Florida	**East South Central**	**Pacific**
Georgia	Alabama	Alaska
Maryland	Kentucky	California
North Carolina	Mississippi	Hawaii
South Carolina	Tennessee	Oregon
Virginia		Washington
West Virginia		

The third largest region was the South Atlantic, which, unlike the Mid-Atlantic and East North Central regions, experienced a small increase from 1988 to 1995; 13.7 percent in 1988 to 14.6 percent in 1991 to 15.1 percent (17,061) in 1995.

Geographic Region, by Degree

One might assume that the proportion of BSWs, MSWs, and PhD–DSWs would be about the same from one region to the next. This assumption does not hold up. An examination of geographic region in relation to the type of degree held by NASW members shows a higher proportion of BSWs who work in the central states.

In 1995, 5.8 percent of the respondents resided in the West North Central region, but a disproportionate 13.4 percent of the 6,554 BSW members who responded lived there. A disproportionately high number

61

TABLE 3.11

Percentage of Working NASW Members, by Regional Distribution

Region	1988	1991	1995
East North Central	19.3	18.8	18.5
East South Central	2.9	3.0	3.4
Mid-Atlantic	24.2	23.2	22.8
Mountain	4.2	4.6	5.0
New England	10.6	10.5	10.4
Pacific	12.2	12.3	11.7
South Atlantic	13.7	14.6	15.1
Territories	0.1	0.1	0.3
West South Central	6.3	6.5	7.0
West North Central	6.4	6.4	5.8
Total respondents	85,712	100,547	113,186

of BSW members were also found in the East North Central, East South Central, West South Central, and Mountain regions. However, there were disproportionately fewer BSW members in the New England, Mid-Atlantic, and Mountain regions. BSWs were an approximately equal proportion of the total NASW membership only in the South Atlantic and West South Central regions (see Table 3.12).

Because the proportions of MSWs and PhD–DSWs in each region were roughly equivalent to the proportion of NASW members residing in each region in 1995, the disparities at the BSW level may point to untested differences in the job market for BSW graduates in the regions. For example, it is possible that in regions other than New England and North Central, where the nonprofit sector is most firmly entrenched, social services are provided primarily by the public sector, which tends to employ proportionately more BSW members than do other sectors (see chapter 4). There may be more employment opportunities for BSW social workers in these regions.

EXPERIENCE

There was a downward trend in the level of experience of NASW members from 1988 to 1995. The median level of experience was 11 to 15 years in both 1991 and 1995 versus 16 to 20 years in 1988 (see Table 3.13).

TABLE 3.12

Percentage of Working NASW Members, by Highest Degree and
Region, 1995

Region	BSW	MSW	PhD–DSW
East North Central	24.2	18.3	14.9
East South Central	7.9	3.1	3.2
Mid-Atlantic	10.6	23.5	26.4
Mountain	7.7	4.9	5.3
New England	5.3	10.8	9.2
Pacific	4.5	12.2	11.3
South Atlantic	15.2	15.0	16.8
Territories	0.2	0.3	0.5
West North Central	13.4	5.3	5.9
West South Central	10.8	6.8	6.4
Total respondents	6,554	101,222	4,576
Percent of total	5.8	90.1	4.1

Note: N = 112,352.

TABLE 3.13

Percentage of Working NASW Members, by Years of Experience

Experience in Years	1988	1991	1995	Percentage Change 1991–1995
Less than 2	0.2	11.1	13.1	2.0
2–5	7.7	17.4	16.5	– 0.9
6–10	9.4	16.4	19.6	3.2
11–15	23.7	18.9	19.5	0.6
16–20	23.6	15.8	14.8	– 1.0
21–25	16.6	10.6	9.3	– 1.3
More than 25	18.8	9.8	7.2	– 2.6
Total respondents	49,945	84,792	86,132	

Approximately 76 percent (86,132) of the total 1995 data set of employed NASW members responded to the question about experience. In 1995, 49.2 percent (42,348) of the respondents indicated that they had 10 or fewer years of experience, up from 44.9 percent in 1991 and in sharp contrast to 17.3 percent in 1988. There was also a sharp contrast between the higher levels of experience between 1988 and 1995. In 1995, 31.3 percent (26,950) of respondents had 16 or more years of experience compared with 36.2 percent in 1991 and 59.0 percent in 1988. Although there was an increase in the experience level of respondents between 1991 and 1995, it is relatively small compared with the downward direction since 1988.

These data are consistent with findings concerning date of highest social work degree. There, we saw that the largest category of respondents (numerically and proportionally) had recently earned their highest social work degree. In 1995, 13.1 percent (11,284) of respondents had less than two years of experience compared with 11.1 percent in 1991 and 0.2 percent in 1988.

Years of Experience, by Highest Social Work Degree

As Table 3.14 shows, the NASW membership was less experienced in 1995 than in 1988. For example, in 1988, 62.3 percent of the respondents whose highest social work degree was a BSW had five or fewer years of experience compared with 81.7 percent in 1991 and 69.3 percent in 1995. For those with MSW degrees, 8.4 percent reported five or fewer years of experience in 1988 versus 29.6 percent in 1991 and 29.2 percent in 1995.

The proportion of members with more than 15 years of experience, at all degree levels, has steadily declined. In 1988, 57.6 percent of responding MSW members had more than 15 years of experience compared with 34.5 percent in 1991 and 30.6 percent in 1995. For those at the PhD–DSW level, there has been a similar decrease in the proportion of more experienced members. In 1988, 83.3 percent of responding PhD–DSW members had more than 15 years of experience versus 73.2 percent in 1991 and 62.9 percent in 1995.

The most experienced NASW respondents were those with doctoral degrees. For example, in 1995, 40.8 percent of responding PhD or DSW members had more than 20 years of experience compared with 15.7 percent of the MSW members and 4.1 percent of the BSW members. This finding is not surprising because doctoral-level members tend to be

TABLE 3.14

Percentage of Working NASW Members, by Years of Experience and Highest Degree

Experience in Years	BSW			MSW			PhD–DSW		
	1988	1991	1995	1988	1991	1995	1988	1991	1995
Less than 2	5.4	63.6	46.8	0.3	11.6	12.4	0.0	0.6	2.0
2–5	56.9	18.1	22.5	8.1	18.0	16.8	0.8	3.3	5.5
6–10	13.7	8.8	14.2	9.8	16.8	20.2	2.4	6.5	11.2
11–15	10.6	4.0	8.4	24.3	19.1	20.1	13.4	16.5	18.3
16–20	5.1	2.3	4.1	23.6	15.4	14.9	24.5	25.4	22.1
21–25	5.6	2.1	1.8	16.3	10.1	9.0	21.6	21.0	20.2
More than 25	2.7	1.1	2.3	17.7	9.0	6.7	37.2	26.7	20.6
Total respondents	663	1,791	3,015	46,655	80,859	78,870	2,890	3,833	3,806
Percent of total	5.0	3.3	3.5	93.7	94.6	92.0	1.3	2.1	4.4

older than MSW- or BSW-level members and age is positively associated with experience.

Experience, by Date of Highest Social Work Degree

When experience is analyzed in relation to the date of receipt of the highest social work degree, the findings also show a predictable trend. The respondents who earned their degrees in earlier years had more experience in 1995. Of those who earned their highest degrees between 1986 and 1990, 40 percent (6,940 of 17,351 respondents) had two to five years of experience. Of those who earned their highest degree between 1976 and 1980, 45.6 percent (6,369) had 11 to 15 years of experience. And, of those who earned their highest degree between 1961 and 1970, 78.8 percent (6,524) had 21 to 25 years of experience.

Experience, by Gender

When experience is examined in relation to gender, the findings again reveal expected patterns. Because a higher proportion of male members were age 41 and older in 1995, it is not surprising that men were generally more experienced. Indeed, the proportion of women with 10 or fewer years of experience was consistently higher than the proportion of men in each years-of-experience category (under two years, two to five years, and so on) whereas the proportion of men was approximately equal to that of women in the category of 11 to 15 years of experience and substantially higher than that of women with 16 or more years of experience.

CHAPTER HIGHLIGHTS

- The proportion of members employed part-time increased.
- The proportion of women members increased.
- The largest proportion of male members were age 41 to 60, compared with age 35 to 50 for female members.
- Compared with the membership as a whole, women were disproportionately represented among those with a BSW as their highest degree and men were disproportionately represented among those with a PhD–DSW as their highest degree.
- There were proportionately fewer African American male members and more Chicano male members than those of other ethnic groups in the NASW membership.

- The NASW membership was overwhelmingly white.
- The proportion of people of color within the NASW membership remained basically unchanged between 1988 and 1995.
- The proportion of people of color who are NASW members lagged behind the proportion of people of color who have social work degrees.
- The median age of NASW members remained consistent at 41 to 45.
- Those whose highest social work degree is the BSW tended to be the youngest members.
- The trend toward a younger population of NASW members was also evident at the doctoral level.
- More than 90 percent of the employed NASW membership had an MSW as their highest social work degree.
- Approximately 4 percent of the members were at the doctoral level.
- In absolute and proportional numbers, BSWs were underrepresented in the membership compared with the number of BSW degrees awarded.
- A significant proportion of members joined NASW soon after they received their highest degree.
- A significant number of members ceased to be members after several years of membership.
- The highest proportion of members lived, in rank order, in the Mid-Atlantic, East North Central, and South Atlantic regions.
- The proportion of MSWs and PhD–DSWs in each region was approximately equivalent to the proportion of members residing in each region.
- The proportion of BSW members in each region did not mirror their proportion in the NASW membership.
- The level of experience of NASW members decreased.
- Doctoral-level members had the most years of experience.

REFERENCES

Becker, R. (1961). *Study of salaries of NASW members.* New York: National Association of Social Workers.

Lennon, T. (1995). *Statistics on social work education in the United States: 1994.* Washington, DC: Council on Social Work Education.

Spaulding, E. (1991). *Statistics on social work education in the United States: 1990.* Alexandria, VA: Council on Social Work Education.

CHAPTER 4

WHERE WE WORK

AUSPICE AND SETTING

PRIMARY AUSPICE

NASW delineates six categories for the auspice, or operating authority, of social work practice: public local, public state, public federal, public military, private not-for-profit, and private for-profit. (Data collection forms predating 1994 distinguished between private not-for-profit sectarian and nonsectarian auspices.) NASW members are asked to indicate, from these categories, the auspice under which they work.

Social work practice is predominantly carried out under the aegis of public, not-for-profit, and for-profit organizations. Private not-for-profit continues to be the first-ranked auspice of NASW members. In 1995, 38.4 percent (33,465) of the 87,196 respondents to this question identified private not-for-profit as the auspice under which they work, down slightly from 38.9 percent in 1991 and 39.8 percent in 1988. Public auspices at the combined local, state, federal, and military levels ranked second, representing 33.7 percent (29,421) of respondents in 1995, down significantly from 37.2 percent in 1991 and 40.4 percent in 1988 (see Table 4.1). Government downsizing has become a major political theme, echoed by both the Democrats and Republicans, in recent years.

In contrast, the proportion of respondents who worked under private for-profit auspices increased between 1988 and 1995—from 19.8 percent in 1988 to 23.8 percent in 1991 and 27.9 percent (24,310) in 1995. As shown in Figure 4.1, there is a consistent trend of social workers moving away from public and not-for-profit organizations at slightly more than 1.0 percent per year. Between 1988 and 1995, the percentage of NASW members working in public and not-for-profit auspices declined by 8.0 percent, with the largest decline (7.0 percent)

TABLE 4.1

Primary Auspice of Working NASW Members

Auspice	1988 n	1988 %	1991 n	1991 %	1995 n	1995 %
Private for-profit	13,223	19.8	19,753	23.8	24,310	27.9
Private not-for-profit	26,623	39.8	32,246	38.9	33,465	38.4
Public federal	2,185	3.3	2,399	2.9	2,330	2.7
Public local	12,309	18.4	15,368	18.5	14,945	17.1
Public military	513	0.8	653	0.8	787	0.9
Public state	11,937	17.9	12,461	15.0	11,359	13.0
Total respondents	66,790		82,880		87,196	

occurring in the public sector. During the same period, the percentage of NASW members working in for-profit organizations (including independent practice) increased by the same 8.0 percent.

Rankings by individual categories for the three study years were consistent: private not-for-profit, private for-profit, and public local ranked first, second, and third, respectively. The growing proportion of NASW members employed by private for-profit organizations suggests that, contrary to historical patterns, the for-profit sector has evolved into a major employer of social workers. This rise in for-profit employment may be attributed, in part, to changes in regulations that have opened the door to third-party payments and vendorship for social work practitioners and, in part, to the growth in purchase-of-service contracting between government and not-for-profit and for-profit service providers. It is possible, however, that some respondents did not accurately distinguish for-profit and not-for-profit auspices because they were not familiar with these terms.

Primary Auspice, by Highest Social Work Degree

A respondent's primary auspice differed to some extent according to highest level of social work education. For example, in 1995, the largest proportion of BSW respondents, 41.6 percent (1,301 of 3,129 respondents), identified government (federal, state, local, or military) as their primary auspice (Table 4.2). However, there have been significant

FIGURE 4.1

Trends in Primary Auspice of Working NASW Members

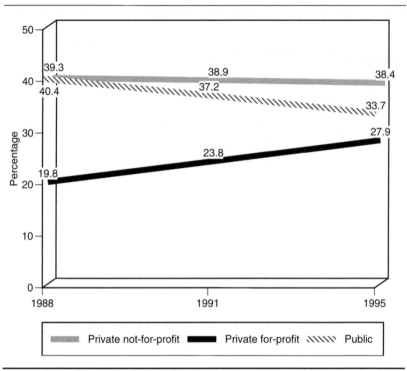

changes in auspice since 1991, when 25.3 percent of responding BSW members, compared with 21.4 percent in 1995, cited public local (government) as their primary auspice. In chapter 7, the impact of the declassification of social services positions is discussed as one explanation for the diminished number of professionally trained social workers in the public social services. In 1991, 24.2 percent of BSW respondents, compared with 40.4 percent in 1995, identified the private not-for-profit sector as their primary auspice of practice.

The primary auspice of the majority of MSW respondents was the private not-for-profit sector at 38.6 percent (30,782 of 79,649 respondents), followed by the private for-profit sector at 28.3 percent (22,547) and local government at 17.3 percent (13,804). The largest growth area has been in the for-profit sector, up from 24.3 percent in 1991.

Where We Work

TABLE 4.2

Percentage of Working NASW Members, by Primary Auspice and Degree, 1995

Auspice	BSW	MSW	Phd–DSW
Private for-profit	18.1	28.3	27.5
Private not-for-profit[a]	40.4	38.6	31.6
Public federal	2.7	2.7	2.4
Public local	21.4	17.3	9.4
Public military	0.7	0.9	1.3
Public state	16.8	12.1	27.9
Total respondents	3,129	79,649	3,912
Percent of total	3.6	91.9	4.5

Note: N = 86,690.
[a]Private not-for-profit sectarian was combined with private not-for-profit in 1995.

In 1995, the largest proportion of doctoral-level members were employed in the private not-for-profit sector, a change from 1991 when state government ranked first. Still, 27.9 percent (1,092 of 3,912 respondents) of PhD–DSW members identified state government as their primary auspice of practice, perhaps reflecting faculty status at publicly supported universities. The third highest proportion of doctoral-level members, 27.5 percent (1,075), worked under private for-profit auspices. This finding may reflect a relatively large number of PhD–DSW members in private solo or group practice or, as with state government, teaching at private universities.

It is interesting that the highest proportion of the respondents who worked under military auspices in 1995 were PhD–DSWs, a pattern consistent with that of earlier years. Although the total number employed by the military was relatively small, there was a discernible bias toward those holding a doctorate, perhaps because of financial support provided by the military to pursue doctoral studies.

Primary Auspice, by Years of Experience

Two patterns can be observed when examining the experience of NASW members by the auspice of their primary employment. First, the distribution of working members by auspice reinforces the assertion that the NASW membership has become less experienced since 1988.

71

For every auspice, there was a significant increase between 1988 and 1995 in the percentage of members with less experience. Second, there was an identifiable pattern of less-experienced members working with traditional agency-based clients. In 1995, the largest proportion of respondents in most auspices had six to 10 years of experience, down from 11 to 15 years in 1991. Deviating from this pattern were the public local and private not-for-profit auspices, in which the largest proportion of respondents (33.1 and 33.8 percent, respectively) had five or fewer years of experience (see Table 4.3).

Primary Auspice, by Age

Patterns in relation to primary auspice and age are similar to those found for experience and age. The vast majority of those working in the private for-profit sector are over age 40, whereas those working in the not-for-profit sector are concentrated in the under-40 categories. Similarly, members employed by the federal government tend to be older than 40, whereas those working in local government are concentrated in the under-40 age groups. These findings are consistent for secondary auspice by age.

Primary Auspice, by Date of Highest Degree

Findings in regard to primary auspice and date of highest degree are also consistent with those of primary auspice and age and experience. The largest proportion of those working in the private for-profit sector in 1995 earned their highest degree between 1971 and 1985. Those working in the not-for-profit sector tended to earn their highest degree later, after 1981. State and federal government employees tend to earn their degrees earlier. However, for local government employees, there are no consistent patterns. Findings are consistent in regard to secondary auspice and date of highest degree. Most recent graduates (1990 or later) are overrepresented in the private not-for-profit sector and at all levels of government except the military. In contrast, those with a secondary auspice of private for-profit tend to be members with an earlier degree date.

Primary Auspice, by Gender

A higher proportion of men (38.3 percent, or 7,696 of 20,098 respondents) than women (32.4 percent, or 21,324 of 65,710 respondents) cited government (at the local, state, federal, or military level) as their primary auspice in 1995. This finding is consistent with the

TABLE 4.3

Percentage of Working NASW Members, by Primary Auspice and
Years of Experience

	Primary Auspice					
Years	Public Local	Public State	Public Federal	Public Military	Private Not-for-Profit	Private for-Profit
Less than 2						
1988	0.3	0.2	0.6	0.9	0.2	0.2
1991	12.0	9.9	7.1	6.1	10.4	6.0
1995	15.4	13.3	13.2	10.5	14.6	7.2
2–5						
1988	9.9	6.0	6.2	7.4	8.2	5.0
1991	20.9	14.4	14.0	15.9	20.5	12.5
1995	17.7	14.3	13.1	16.2	19.2	12.8
6–10						
1988	10.4	6.4	6.3	11.2	9.0	8.0
1991	15.9	14.0	12.0	16.6	17.7	17.7
1995	19.3	17.1	15.3	19.1	20.3	20.5
11–15						
1988	21.1	21.5	18.4	24.7	23.0	25.9
1991	16.7	18.5	18.0	21.8	18.0	23.8
1995	18.4	18.7	16.7	21.6	18.3	23.2
16–20						
1988	22.3	25.0	26.0	29.7	22.5	26.5
1991	14.6	17.8	19.1	22.3	14.1	19.0
1995	13.8	16.4	18.5	17.7	12.9	18.0
21–25						
1988	17.7	19.1	19.0	15.9	15.8	17.5
1991	10.8	13.2	14.9	11.3	9.5	11.8
1995	8.9	11.3	13.5	10.2	8.0	10.6
More than 25						
1988	18.2	21.8	23.5	10.3	21.3	16.9
1991	9.2	12.2	14.8	5.9	9.9	9.3
1995	6.6	9.0	9.7	4.7	6.7	7.7

proportionately higher salaries offered by government and the higher
salaries earned by male NASW members (see chapter 6). However, as
noted earlier, overall member employment in government has decreased
substantially since 1988, and gender differences have also narrowed in

regard to this auspice of employment. The proportion of women was higher in the private not-for-profit and private for-profit primary auspices, a trend also consistent over time (see Table 4.4).

Distinctions on the basis of gender were less notable for the secondary auspice than for the primary auspice. The proportion of men with a secondary auspice of private for-profit was higher than for women—52.6 percent versus 49.4 percent, a reversal of the pattern for the primary auspice.

Primary Auspice, by Ethnicity

An examination of primary auspice in relation to the ethnicity of NASW members revealed some interesting patterns. In 1995, a significantly higher proportion of people of color than of white people among the NASW membership were employed by the local, state, or federal government. Furthermore, there were some distinctions based on the level of government. For example, a higher proportion of Asian and African American members than other ethnic groups cited state government as their primary auspice. African American, Chicano, Puerto Rican, and Other Hispanic members had a higher ratio of employment in state government. A significantly higher proportion of Native Americans cited the federal government as their primary auspice than did those of other ethnic groups. White members and members of mixed heritage were overrepresented in the private for-profit sector. Puerto Ricans, white

TABLE 4.4

Working NASW Members, by Primary Auspice and Gender, 1995

	Female		Male		Total Respondents	
Auspice	n	%	n	%	n	%
Private for-profit	18,786	28.6	5,063	25.2	23,849	27.8
Private not-for-profit	25,600	39.0	7,339	36.5	32,939	38.4
Private total	44,386	67.6	12,402	61.7	56,788	66.2
Public federal	1,435	2.2	856	4.3	2,291	2.7
Public local	11,310	17.2	3,457	17.2	14,767	17.2
Public military	471	0.7	307	1.5	778	0.9
Public state	8,108	12.3	3,076	15.3	11,184	13.0
Public total	21,324	32.4	7,696	38.3	29,020	33.8
Total	65,710	76.6	20,098	23.4	85,808	100.0

people, and members of mixed heritage represented a higher proportion of those in the private not-for-profit sector (see Table 4.5). As was noted, the for-profit sector ranked first among the respondents who cited a secondary auspice. In this category, however, the white respondents had the highest proportional representation of all the ethnic groups.

Primary Auspice, by Function

A few notable patterns emerge in the relationship between primary auspice and primary and secondary function. A disproportionate number of members who worked under private not-for-profit and military auspices in 1995 cited administration–management as their primary function compared with members working under other auspices. Although 15.8 percent of the respondents to both questions (auspice and function) perform an administrative function, 23.2 percent of those in the not-for-profit sector and 20.5 percent of those in the military report administration as their primary function (see Table 4.6). Also, of those performing an administrative function, 56.3 percent are found in the not-for-profit sector.

NASW members employed by state governments reported proportionately fewer members who cited a primary function of clinical practice, although 53.6 percent of those working in state government did report clinical–direct service as their primary function.

Respondents working for military, federal, or state government tended to be involved in policy practice more than their counterparts employed under other auspices. Similarly, a disproportionate number of members with federal or state government auspices held primary functions in research. Still, the fewest number and lowest percentage of NASW members reported a primary function in these two areas and in the area of training (see chapter 5 for further discussion).

Supervision as a primary function is underrepresented in the private for-profit sector compared with other auspices of practice. This finding may hold implications for the nature and conditions of work in that sector.

Finally, state government is a major employer of members engaged in the primary function of teaching, probably reflecting the number of public colleges and universities in which social work educators work.

Findings in regard to primary auspice by secondary function are similar to those of primary auspice by primary function. A disproportionate number of members employed by the military engaged in

TABLE 4.5

Percentage of Working NASW Members, by Primary Auspice and Ethnicity, 1995

Auspice	Native American	Asian	African American	Chicano	Puerto Rican	Other Hispanic	White	Mixed Heritage	Other	Number of Respondents	Percentage in Auspice
Private for-profit	0.4	1.0	2.1	0.7	0.4	0.7	93.7	1.0	0.1	22,162	27.6
Private not-for-profit	0.4	1.7	4.1	0.8	0.9	1.0	89.9	1.1	0.1	30,846	38.5
Public federal	2.7	2.3	11.7	1.3	0.7	1.1	79.0	1.1	0.0	2,137	2.7
Public local	0.5	2.0	8.6	1.7	1.1	1.5	83.2	1.3	0.1	13,807	17.2
Public military	0.4	2.9	11.9	1.4	1.2	1.1	79.7	1.5	0.0	734	0.9
Public state	0.7	2.9	8.9	1.1	0.9	1.1	83.0	1.3	0.0	10,466	13.1
Total respondents	416	1,422	4,182	799	631	796	70,926	928	52	80,152	
Percent of total	0.5	1.8	5.2	1.0	0.8	1.0	88.5	1.2	0.1		100.0

TABLE 4.6

Percentage of Working NASW Members, by Primary Auspice and Primary Function, 1995

Function	Auspice						Number of Respondents	Percentage in Function
	Public Local	Public State	Public Federal	Public Military	Private Not-for-Profit	Private for-Profit		
Administration	13.1	17.8	17.4	20.5	23.2	6.2	13,593	15.8
Community organizing	0.2	0.4	0.0	0.4	0.4	0.1	225	0.3
Direct service	72.0	53.6	66.1	64.4	63.2	87.6	60,410	70.3
Policy	0.9	1.8	1.9	2.1	0.8	0.2	689	0.8
Research	0.1	1.4	1.9	0.3	0.4	0.1	376	0.4
Supervision	7.8	8.1	7.2	6.3	6.6	1.2	4,836	5.6
Teaching	3.9	13.8	2.2	3.6	3.3	0.8	3,450	4.0
Training	0.0	0.1	0.1	0.1	0.1	0.0	62	0.1
Other	2.1	3.0	3.2	2.3	1.9	3.8	2,241	2.6
Total respondents	14,726	11,176	2,287	779	33,026	23,888	85,882	
Percent of total	17.1	13.0	2.7	0.9	38.5	27.8		100.0

administration–management compared with those working under other auspices. Clinical practice is underrepresented as a secondary function for those employed in the private for-profit sector. For those working for the federal or state government, policy and research, as secondary functions, are overrepresented. And a disproportionate number of members who cited the private for-profit sector as their secondary auspice of practice held teaching positions; this finding may relate to the reliance of private colleges and universities on adjunct faculty.

Primary Auspice, by Primary Setting

The respondents' auspice affects, and is affected by, the primary setting of practice. For example, those employed under the auspice of the military or local government are more likely to cite outpatient health as their primary setting of practice. Military personnel are also more likely to cite outpatient mental health as their primary setting of practice. Members working in the military or federal government are more likely to have a primary practice setting of inpatient health (see Table 4.7). This latter finding may reflect the proportion of government employees working in Veterans Administration Hospitals or armed forces hospitals, such as the Walter Reed Army Medical Center in Washington, DC.

Not surprisingly, members working for state and local governments are disproportionately represented among those with a primary practice setting of the courts–justice system. Also not surprising is the positive relationship between the private for-profit sector and the primary settings of private group and private solo practice. Those working under for-profit auspices are also less likely to cite social services agencies as their primary practice setting.

SECONDARY AUSPICE

The trend away from the traditional government and not-for-profit bases of social work practice and toward the private for-profit sector was pronounced in relation to the secondary auspice. Of the 24,035 respondents who identified a secondary auspice in 1995, 50.4 percent (12,113) reported the auspice to be private for-profit. These findings are consistent with data from earlier years: In 1991, 49.6 percent of respondents and in 1988, 49.0 percent of respondents identified their secondary auspice as private for-profit. This category may include both organizational settings and individual or group private practice (see Figure 4.2).

TABLE 4.7

Percentage of Working NASW Members, by Primary Auspice and Primary Setting, 1995

Setting	Public Local	Public State	Public Federal	Auspice Public Military	Private Not-for-Profit	Private for-Profit	Number of Respondents	Percentage in Setting
Business–industry	0.0	0.0	0.1	0.5	0.1	0.5	143	0.2
Colleges–universities	1.4	17.2	2.2	1.1	3.4	0.6	3,361	4.0
Courts–justice system	3.3	4.1	2.3	1.4	0.4	0.1	1,139	1.4
Health (inpatient)	10.9	17.6	50.8	32.6	22.7	11.8	14,966	17.8
Health (outpatient)	22.1	13.2	18.4	25.9	20.0	7.9	13,551	16.1
Managed care	0.0	0.1	0.0	0.1	0.2	0.6	226	0.3
Mental health (inpatient)	0.2	1.7	0.6	1.4	0.7	0.7	644	0.8
Mental health (outpatient)	2.1	1.4	2.1	5.1	3.6	1.7	2,131	2.5
Private group	0.3	0.2	0.6	0.3	1.1	17.0	4,422	5.3
Private solo	0.8	0.6	0.9	0.3	1.8	48.4	12,157	14.4
Residential facility	2.8	7.7	3.6	2.8	10.0	4.6	5,678	6.7
School (preschool–grade 12)	28.0	7.4	2.3	1.3	2.3	0.3	5,761	6.8
Social services agency	26.8	26.9	11.5	18.8	30.4	1.5	17,390	20.7
Other	1.2	1.7	4.6	8.3	3.3	4.3	2,579	3.1
Total respondents	14,589	10,769	2,251	760	32,290	23,489	84,148	
Percent of total	17.3	12.8	2.7	0.9	38.4	27.9		100.0

The second-ranked secondary auspice in the three study years was the not-for-profit sector. In 1995, 29.2 percent (7,029) of members responding to this question reported that they worked under not-for-profit auspices. Similar proportions were found in 1991 (28.4 percent) and 1988 (28.6 percent).

The third-ranked auspice for the three study years was local government at 9.3 percent (2,232) in 1995, 9.9 percent in 1991, and 9.8 percent in 1988. The number of social workers who identified a public secondary auspice is surprising because the government is not typically a secondary employer. In 1995, 20.4 percent (4,893) of NASW members who responded to the question identified their secondary auspice of practice as public. It is possible that a significant proportion of these members provide consultation or contract services.

FIGURE 4.2

Secondary Auspice of Working NASW Members

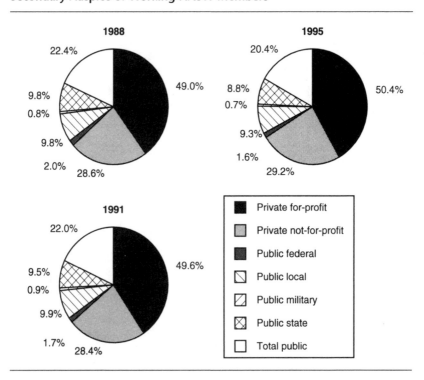

Secondary Auspice, by Highest Degree Held

When the secondary auspice is examined in relation to the highest degree held, more information is available about the members who identified government as their secondary auspice. The largest proportion of respondents who identified any level of government as their secondary auspice was at the BSW level. For example, 19.7 percent of the BSW respondents listed public local government as their secondary auspice versus 9.2 percent of the MSW respondents and 6.3 percent of the PhD–DSW respondents. The secondary auspice of public state government was identified by 21.9 percent of the BSW respondents compared with 8.3 percent of the MSW respondents and 11.9 percent of the PhD–DSW respondents. Similar findings for the secondary auspice of federal government and military reveal a significantly higher proportion of BSW respondents than MSW or PhD–DSW respondents (see Figure 4.3).

The proportion of respondents whose secondary auspice was private for-profit is noteworthy. In 1995, the private for-profit sector ranked first as the secondary auspice for MSW and PhD–DSW level respondents, with MSWs at 51.3 percent and PhD–DSWs at 47.8 percent. The for-profit sector was the second largest category for BSWs as well, following closely behind state government at 20.2 percent.

Secondary Auspice, by Ethnicity

An examination of secondary auspice in relation to the ethnicity of NASW members revealed some variations from primary auspice by ethnicity. In 1995, a significantly higher proportion of people of color than of white people among the NASW membership identified their secondary auspice as the private not-for-profit sector. White members, similar to findings for primary auspice, were underrepresented compared with people of color at all levels of government. A higher proportion of Native Americans, compared with all other ethnic groups, identified their secondary auspice as the military or federal government. Compared with the secondary auspice of other ethnic groups, a larger proportion of Asian and Chicano members worked in state government, and African American and Puerto Rican members were overrepresented in local government. White members, Other Hispanic members, and members of mixed heritage were overrepresented in the private for-profit sector. Asian, African American, and Chicano members represented a higher proportion of those in the private not-for-profit sector (see Table 4.8).

FIGURE 4.3

Percentage of Working NASW Members, by Secondary Auspice
and Highest Degree, 1995

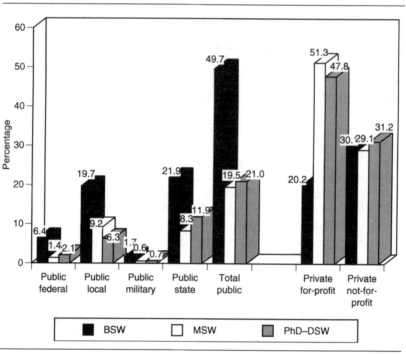

PRIMARY SETTING OF PRACTICE

Of the 14 settings of social work practice identified by NASW, social
services agencies ranked first in all three study years. However, the
proportion of members working in social services agencies has steadily
declined. Of the 88,544 members responding to the question about
primary setting of practice in 1995, 20.5 percent (18,165) identified
social services agencies as their primary setting of practice compared
with 22.8 percent in 1991 and 24.4 percent in 1988 (see Table 4.9).
Inpatient health (formerly "hospital") ranked second in the three study
years, at 18.0 percent (15,896) in 1995, 20.9 percent in 1991, and 20.7
percent of the respondents in 1988. Outpatient health (formerly
"clinic") was the third-ranked category in all three years, at 16.2

TABLE 4.8

Percentage of Working NASW Members, by Secondary Auspice and Ethnicity, 1995

Auspice	Native American	Asian	African American	Ethnicity Chicano	Puerto Rican	Other Hispanic	White	Mixed Heritage	Other	Number of Respondents	Percentage in Auspice
Private for-profit	0.4	1.2	3.6	0.8	0.8	1.0	90.8	1.3	0.1	11,145	50.4
Private not-for-profit	0.5	1.7	5.7	1.2	0.9	0.9	87.3	1.6	0.1	6,456	29.2
Public federal	3.1	2.0	9.5	1.1	0.6	1.1	80.7	2.0	0.0	357	1.6
Public local	0.7	1.3	7.6	1.1	1.3	1.2	85.4	1.3	0.1	2,058	9.3
Public military	2.0	2.0	13.5	1.4	0.7	1.4	79.1	0.0	0.0	148	0.7
Public state	0.8	2.3	6.9	1.6	1.1	1.4	84.5	1.3	0.1	1,953	8.8
Total respondents	121	328	1,108	232	193	236	19,572	306	21	22,117	
Percent of total	0.5	1.5	5.0	1.0	0.9	1.1	88.5	1.4	0.1		100.0

percent in 1995 and 17.1 percent in both 1991 and 1988. The decrease in the proportion of NASW members working in outpatient and inpatient health facilities may reflect the downsizing occurring in hospitals and medical clinics throughout the country.

When private solo and private group practice are combined into one category, private practice becomes the second-ranked primary setting of practice. There is a consistent and strong upward trend in the proportion

TABLE 4.9

Percentage of Working NASW Members, by Primary Setting

Setting	1988	1991	1995
Business–industry[a]			0.2
Clinic[b]	17.1	17.1	
Colleges–universities	5.0	4.3	4.1
Courts–justice system	1.4	1.4	1.3
Group home[c]	2.2	2.3	
Health (inpatient)[a]			18.0
Health (outpatient)[a]			16.2
Hospital[d]	20.7	20.9	
Institution[c]	3.1	2.9	
Managed care[a]			0.3
Membership organization[e]	0.8	0.7	
Mental health (inpatient)[a]			0.7
Mental health (outpatient)[a]			2.4
Non–social work[e]	2.4	2.2	
Nursing home[c]	2.1	2.3	
Private group	4.4	4.6	5.2
Private solo	10.4	12.2	14.5
Residential facility[a]			6.7
School (preschool–grade 12)	5.9	6.2	6.8
Social services agency	24.4	22.8	20.5
Other[a]			3.1
Total respondents	66,887	86,006	88,544

[a] This is a new category for 1995.
[b] Category is combined with Health (outpatient) in 1995.
[c] Category is combined with Residential facility in 1995.
[d] Category is combined with Health (inpatient) in 1995.
[e] Category is combined with "other" in 1995.

of NASW members with a primary setting of solo or group private practice. In 1995, 19.7 percent (17,450) of responding members indicated a primary setting of solo or group private practice, up from 16.8 percent in 1991 and 14.8 percent in 1988.

Primary Setting, by Degree

There are significant differences in the primary setting of practice based on the highest degree held. Considerably fewer PhD–DSW respondents than BSW or MSW respondents worked in organizational settings (social services agencies, inpatient health facilities, and the courts) in 1995 (see Table 4.10). The majority worked in universities (37.2 percent) or private solo practice (18.8 percent). This finding confirms earlier hypotheses that members at the doctoral level report their auspice on the basis of the public versus private nature of their employing institutions of higher education.

An examination of the data on primary practice settings reinforces the view that clients with the most complex and intractable socioeconomic and psychosocial problems are served by the least-educated members. Compared with MSWs and PhD–DSWs, more BSWs work in social services agencies, residential facilities, and the courts–justice system, suggesting that they are more likely than others to serve young, old, poor, and mentally and physically disabled people. Proportionally more BSW members are found in "other" settings, and few BSWs work in primary solo or group practice.

Primary Setting, by Date of Highest Social Work Degree

When primary practice settings are examined in relation to the date of receipt of the highest social work degree, some trends, but few startling findings, emerge. There is a tendency for the more recent graduates to work in social services agencies, inpatient and outpatient health facilities, and residential care facilities.

In contrast, those who have been out of school the longest and hence have the greatest amount of experience tend to be in private solo practice, colleges and universities, and schools, whereas the largest proportion of members in private group practice earned their highest degree between 1971 and 1985. These findings suggest that NASW members typically begin their professional practice in organizational settings and then move into private group practice and finally into private solo practice. Findings in regard to secondary setting and date of highest social work degree are similar.

85

TABLE 4.10

Percentage of Working NASW Members, by Primary Setting and Highest Degree, 1995

Setting	BSW	MSW	PhD–DSW
Business–industry[a]	0.2	0.2	0.2
Colleges–universities	2.6	2.6	37.2
Courts–justice system	2.6	1.3	0.6
Health (inpatient)[a]	14.3	18.5	9.7
Health (outpatient)[a]	9.6	16.8	8.5
Managed care[a]	0.5	0.3	0.2
Mental health (inpatient)[a]	0.6	0.8	0.3
Mental health (outpatient)[a]	1.6	2.5	1.3
Private group	1.1	5.4	5.3
Private solo	2.0	14.8	18.8
Residential facility[a]	21.1	6.4	2.2
School (preschool–grade 12)	3.8	7.1	3.2
Social services agency	33.7	20.5	10.1
Other[a]	6.3	3.0	2.5
Total respondents	3,240	80,806	3,968
Percentage	3.7	91.8	4.5

Note: N = 88,014.

[a]These are new or combined former categories for 1995. It may take two or more years before these are accurate representations of the NASW membership.

Trends in regard to secondary practice setting are consistent with those of primary setting. Members who received their highest social work degree in 1985 or earlier tended to cite private solo practice as their secondary practice setting. Members also tended to enter private solo practice sooner after graduation as a secondary rather than primary practice setting.

Primary Setting, by Years of Experience

When the years of experience of NASW members are viewed in relation to primary practice setting, the patterns are similar to those found for the date of receipt of the highest social work degree. Of those who responded to the questions about experience and primary setting in 1995 (81,405), the largest group, 20.1 percent (16,333), reported social services agencies as their primary setting, down from 22.2 percent in 1991. Of those who worked in social services agencies, 55.8 percent had less than 10 years of experience. Other organizational settings demonstrated similarly high proportions of members with less experience.

The more experienced members cited their primary setting as colleges–universities, inpatient and outpatient mental health facilities, and private solo practice. The least experienced members worked in inpatient and outpatient health facilities, residential facilities, and social services agencies (see Table 4.11).

Major shifts in the primary setting of NASW members can be seen at two and five years of experience. In 1995, the proportion of respondents in private group practice increased significantly from 5.4 percent with fewer than two years' experience to 12.6 percent with two to five years' experience (see Table 4.11). Similarly, those in private solo practice increased from 8.6 percent with fewer than five years' experience to 19.5 percent with six to 10 years' experience. All other social work settings experienced a drop in the percentage of respondents reporting six to 10 years of experience compared with those reporting fewer than six years' experience. This is a reversal of the patterns reported by the members in 1988.

The effects of licensing on the practice of social work, at least for NASW members, may account for these shifts in primary setting by experience. NASW's considerable efforts to influence states to adopt professional regulation statutes for social workers have opened the door to private group and solo practice for social workers. In most instances, the laws require two years of supervised experience before semi-independent practice and another two years before unsupervised practice. These requirements correspond to the shifts in settings observed at two and five years of experience in all three data sets.

Primary Setting, by Age

Trends in regard to primary setting and age of NASW members are consistent with those cited earlier for experience and date of highest degree. Those who identified colleges–universities and private solo practice as their primary settings tend to be in the over-40 age group, whereas those with a primary setting of courts–criminal justice system, social services agencies, and residential facilities tend to be younger.

TABLE 4.11

Primary Setting, by Years of Working NASW Members' Experience, 1995

Setting	Years of Experience							Number of Respondents	Percentage in Setting
	Less than 2	2–5	6–10	11–15	16–20	21–25	More than 25		
Business–industry[a]	9.9	13.4	13.4	22.5	16.9	11.3	12.7	142	0.2
Colleges–universities	7.6	7.7	13.0	17.9	20.3	16.4	17.2	3,177	3.9
Courts–justice system	16.1	18.1	19.3	16.0	13.2	10.5	6.7	1,047	1.3
Health (inpatient)[a]	14.2	19.0	21.6	19.3	13.5	7.6	4.8	14,543	17.9
Health (outpatient)[a]	14.3	20.2	21.2	18.6	12.6	7.6	5.4	13,231	16.3
Managed care[a]	10.5	15.8	19.7	19.3	13.6	12.3	8.8	228	0.3
Mental health (inpatient)[a]	11.0	18.3	17.0	16.9	13.3	11.3	12.2	646	0.8
Mental health (outpatient)[a]	10.3	17.9	18.5	18.1	14.9	10.7	9.7	2,151	2.6
Private group	5.4	12.6	21.2	25.3	18.9	10.0	6.7	4,328	5.3
Private solo	1.4	7.2	19.5	26.1	21.8	13.7	10.3	12,181	15.0
Residential facility[a]	21.5	22.3	19.1	15.5	10.3	6.3	4.9	5,354	6.6
School (preschool–grade 12)	11.2	15.2	20.3	21.2	16.0	9.4	6.7	5,557	6.8
Social services agency	18.2	19.2	18.4	16.6	12.4	8.2	7.0	16,333	20.1
Other[a]	15.0	15.4	19.0	19.7	14.4	8.2	8.2	2,487	3.1
Total respondents	10,238	13,397	16,055	16,077	12,160	7,597	5,881	81,405	
Percent of total	12.6	16.5	19.7	19.7	14.9	9.3	7.2		100.0

[a]These are new or combined former categories for 1995. It may take two or more years before these are accurate representations of the NASW membership.

Primary Setting, by Gender

An examination of primary setting of practice in relation to gender reveals only a few distinctive patterns. Following the gender distribution of the general membership, in 1995 the majority of NASW members in all social work settings were women. However, men were overrepresented in colleges–universities, courts–justice system, and mental health (inpatient) and underrepresented in inpatient health facilities, private solo practice, and schools (see Figure 4.4).

Primary Setting, by Ethnicity

When primary setting is examined in relation to ethnicity, the highest proportion of all ethnic groups identified social services agencies as their primary practice setting. Within the category of social services agencies, there is a slightly higher proportion of Native American, Asian, and African American members than members of other ethnic groups. Inpatient health facilities were identified by a higher proportion of African American, Native American, Asian, and Other Hispanic members than those of other ethnic groups, whereas outpatient health facilities were cited by a higher proportion of Chicano, Puerto Rican, and Other Hispanic members (see Table 4.12).

A significantly higher proportion of white respondents cited private solo and private group practice as their primary setting, whereas a higher proportion of people of color identified schools as their primary setting. Native American and white members were overrepresented in residential facilities, and Asian and African American members were overrepresented in colleges and universities compared with those of other ethnic groups.

Primary Setting, by Primary Function

The primary setting of practice affects and is affected by the primary function that NASW members perform. For example, compared with the membership as a whole, significantly smaller proportions of members who cited a primary setting of business–industry, the courts–justice system, managed care, residential facilities, and social services agencies have a primary function of clinical–direct practice; most of them are concentrated in administration–management.

A curious finding is that only 55.5 percent (10,004) of the 18,015 respondents had a primary setting of social services agencies and a primary function of clinical–direct service (see Table 4.13). The

FIGURE 4.4

Percentage of Working NASW Members, by Primary Setting
and Gender, 1995

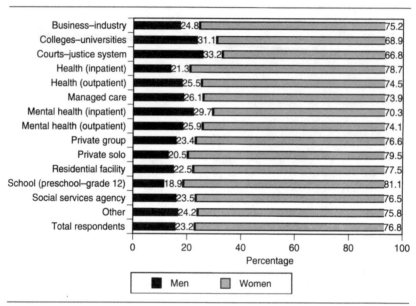

proportion of members working in social services agencies as their
secondary setting of practice and who cited clinical–direct practice as
their primary function is higher, at 65.6 percent, than for those with
social services agencies as their primary setting.

Also compared with the membership as a whole, there is a disproportionately high concentration of members with a primary function
of supervision in the courts–justice system, residential facilities, and
social services agencies. Not surprisingly, members with a primary
setting of colleges–universities are overrepresented among those with a
primary function of research.

Primary Setting, by Primary Practice Area

When primary setting is examined in relation to primary practice area,
there are some discernible, and not surprising, trends. The overwhelming majority of members who cited occupational social work as their

TABLE 4.12

Percentage of Working NASW Members, by Primary Setting and Ethnicity, 1995

Setting	Native American	Asian	African American	Chicano	Puerto Rican	Other Hispanic	White	Mixed Heritage	Other	Number of Respondents	Percentage in Setting
				Ethnicity							
Business–industry[a]	0.0	5.7	2.1	0.7	0.7	2.1	88.7	0.0	0.0	141	0.2
Colleges–universities	0.7	3.8	9.4	1.2	0.9	1.1	81.6	1.4	0.0	3,319	4.1
Courts–justice system	0.9	3.0	8.7	2.1	1.1	1.0	81.3	1.7	0.0	1,088	1.3
Health (inpatient)[a]	0.6	1.8	5.6	0.9	0.8	1.1	88.0	1.1	0.1	14,569	17.9
Health (outpatient)[a]	0.5	1.7	5.0	1.1	1.0	1.1	88.4	1.1	0.0	13,095	16.1
Managed care[a]	0.4	1.3	3.1	1.3	0.4	1.3	89.2	1.8	0.9	223	0.3
Mental health (inpatient)[a]	0.2	3.1	2.8	1.6	0.3	0.9	90.5	0.6	0.0	642	0.8
Mental health (outpatient)[a]	0.4	2.5	2.1	0.9	0.7	1.1	91.1	0.8	0.3	2,132	2.6
Private group	0.5	0.6	1.4	0.9	0.2	0.8	94.8	0.9	0.0	4,198	5.2
Private solo	0.3	0.7	1.2	0.6	0.4	0.6	95.0	1.2	0.1	11,531	14.2
Residential facility[a]	0.6	1.1	5.3	0.6	0.6	0.7	89.9	1.1	0.1	5,477	6.7
School (preschool–grade 12)	0.3	1.5	8.6	1.2	1.6	1.4	83.9	1.3	0.1	5,516	6.8
Social services agency	0.6	2.3	6.8	1.2	0.8	1.1	85.9	1.2	0.1	16,755	20.6
Other[a]	0.6	2.3	6.1	0.9	0.8	0.7	87.3	1.1	0.2	2,593	3.2
Total respondents	428	1,422	4,215	801	645	817	71,964	934	53	81,279	
Percent of total	0.5	1.7	5.2	1.0	0.8	1.0	88.5	1.1	0.1		100.0

[a]These are new or combined former categories for 1995. It may take two or more years before these are accurate representations of the NASW membership.

91

TABLE 4.13

Percentage of Working NASW Members, by Primary Setting and Primary Function, 1995

Setting	Administration	Community Organizing	Clinical–Direct Service	Policy	Research	Supervision	Teaching	Training	Other	Number of Respondents	Percentage in Setting
Business–industry[a]	37.1	0.0	40.6	1.4	0.7	2.8	2.1	2.1	13.3	143	0.2
Colleges–universities	9.2	0.2	14.4	0.8	5.6	1.1	65.6	0.1	3.1	3,614	4.1
Courts–justice system	19.7	0.6	63.2	1.8	0.1	8.6	1.1	0.0	4.9	1,152	1.3
Health (inpatient)[a]	17.2	0.1	74.3	0.4	0.3	5.4	0.8	0.0	1.4	15,777	18.0
Health (outpatient)[a]	15.6	0.3	75.4	0.3	0.1	6.7	0.8	0.0	1.4	14,205	16.2
Managed care[a]	24.2	3.1	55.2	0.4	0.4	2.2	0.0	0.9	13.5	223	0.3
Mental health (inpatient)[a]	21.0	0.8	69.8	0.3	0.3	5.1	0.3	0.6	1.7	643	0.7
Mental health (outpatient)[a]	17.9	0.7	74.8	0.3	0.3	4.8	0.0	0.1	1.0	2,140	2.4
Private group	2.7	0.1	94.6	0.2	0.0	0.6	0.2	0.0	1.6	4,570	5.2
Private solo	0.8	0.1	95.9	0.1	0.1	0.3	0.4	0.0	2.4	12,726	14.5
Residential facility[a]	24.5	0.1	62.1	0.7	0.2	7.3	1.5	0.0	3.6	5,883	6.7
School (preschool–grade 12)	4.3	0.4	82.1	0.3	0.0	1.9	7.6	0.0	3.3	5,943	6.8
Social services agency	26.8	0.3	55.5	1.7	0.3	11.7	1.7	0.2	1.7	18,015	20.5
Other[a]	28.6	1.2	34.5	3.8	1.2	3.6	2.4	0.3	24.4	2,743	3.1
Total respondents	13,652	227	61,919	661	390	4,899	3,613	64	2,352	87,777	
Percent of total	15.6	0.3	70.5	0.8	0.4	5.6	4.1	0.1	2.7		100.0

[a]These are new or combined former categories for 1995. It may take two or more years before these are accurate representations of the NASW membership.

primary practice area worked within the primary setting of business–industry (see Table 4.14). Understandably, criminal justice is primarily carried out in the courts–justice system. The primary settings of private group and private solo practice relate largely to the practice of mental health. A disproportionately large number of members who worked in residential facilities cited aging and criminal justice as their primary practice areas. These relationships were also evident in regard to secondary setting and primary practice.

SECONDARY SETTING OF PRACTICE

Approximately 26 percent (29,392) of the data set of 113,352 employed NASW members in 1995 responded to the question about a secondary setting of practice. The trend toward the private practice of social work is highlighted by the proportion of respondents who indicated private practice, solo or group, as their secondary setting—45.4 percent in 1995 and 45.8 percent in both 1991 and 1988 (see Table 4.15).

Private solo practice ranked first among secondary settings of practice in the three study years, followed by outpatient health, private group practice, and social services agencies, respectively. In 1995, 7.8 percent (2,286) of the respondents identified colleges–universities as their secondary practice setting, consistent with 7.8 percent in 1991 and 7.9 percent in 1988. These data suggest that schools of social work frequently hire practitioners as adjunct faculty for fieldwork supervision or classroom teaching.

Secondary Setting, by Degree

The findings regarding secondary practice setting and primary practice setting by degree are consistent. In 1995, the BSW respondents more frequently than the MSW or PhD–DSW respondents reported social services agencies, the courts–justice system, inpatient health facilities, residential facilities, schools, and "other" as their secondary settings. The majority of MSW respondents with a secondary setting worked in private solo or group practice and clinics—33.6 percent in private solo practice, 12.5 percent in private group practice, and 12.7 percent in outpatient health facilities (see Table 4.16).

The majority of PhD–DSW respondents with a secondary practice setting also worked in private or solo group practice in 1995—34.5 percent in private solo practice and 11.1 percent in private group practice. Colleges and universities were also a major secondary setting for doctoral-level members, at 21.9 percent.

TABLE 4.14

Percentage of Working NASW Members, by Primary Setting and Primary Practice Area, 1995

Setting	Practice Area								Number of Respondents	Percentage in Setting
	Aging	Child-Family	Justice	Medical Health	Mental Health	Occupational Social Work	Schools	Other		
Business-industry[a]	6.5	5.0	0.7	7.9	10.1	50.4	1.4	18.0	139	0.2
Colleges-universities	4.0	16.4	1.1	5.5	20.5	1.8	8.2	42.5	3,137	3.6
Courts-justice system	1.1	27.7	55.1	0.8	6.0	0.1	0.2	9.0	1,152	1.3
Health (inpatient)[a]	3.1	8.9	0.3	45.4	33.6	0.4	0.1	8.3	15,695	18.2
Health (outpatient)[a]	2.3	17.6	0.1	12.7	56.6	0.2	0.1	10.4	14,093	16.4
Managed care[a]	10.2	3.1	0.4	11.9	57.1	7.1	0.4	9.7	226	0.3
Mental health (inpatient)[a]	3.1	3.7	0.8	1.7	88.5	0.3	0.0	1.9	642	0.7
Mental health (outpatient)[a]	2.2	6.3	0.2	0.7	87.0	0.9	0.2	2.5	2,137	2.5
Private group	1.6	19.4	0.2	1.7	68.9	0.8	0.2	7.1	4,501	5.2
Private solo	1.5	16.3	0.3	1.7	73.0	0.4	0.1	6.8	12,478	14.5
Residential facility[a]	20.3	28.3	2.3	15.8	22.6	0.4	0.7	9.6	5,882	6.8
School (preschool-grade 12)	0.2	24.5	0.0	0.1	2.9	0.1	69.0	3.2	5,903	6.8
Social services agency	6.8	57.9	0.5	2.8	16.4	0.6	0.4	14.5	17,633	20.5
Other[a]	7.8	13.7	1.0	10.4	18.6	9.2	0.8	38.6	2,571	3.0
Total respondents	3,905	2,147	1,030	11,149	33,608	698	4,532	9,797	86,189	
Percent of total	4.5	24.9	1.2	12.9	39.0	0.8	5.3	11.4		100.0

[a]These are new or combined former categories for 1995. It may take two or more years before these are accurate representations of the NASW membership.

TABLE 4.15

Secondary Setting of Working NASW Members

Setting	1988 n	1988 %	1991 n	1991 %	1995 n	1995 %
Business–industry[a]					35	0.1
Clinic		12.5		12.7		[b]
Colleges–universities	1,738	7.9	2,177	7.8	2,286	7.8
Courts–justice system	390	1.8	460	1.6	488	1.7
Group home		2.6		2.7		[c]
Health (inpatient)[a]	1,451	6.6	2,064	7.4	2,141	7.3
Health (outpatient)[a]	2,758	12.5	3,545	12.7	3,612	12.3
Hospital		6.6		7.4		[d]
Institution		2.1		2.1		[c]
Managed care[a]					46	0.2
Membership organization		0.9		1.0		[e]
Mental health (inpatient)[a]					94	0.3
Mental health (outpatient)[a]					496	1.7
Non–social work		4.3		3.3		[e]
Nursing home		3.6		3.3		[c]
Private group	2,691	12.2	3,461	12.4	3,601	12.3
Private solo	7,396	33.6	9,325	33.4	9,722	33.1
Residential facility[a]	1,836	8.4	2,225	8.0	2,093	7.1
School (preschool–grade 12)	475	2.2	716	2.6	819	2.8
Social services agency	2,103	9.6	2,815	10.1	2,839	9.7
Other[a]	1,149	5.2	1,148	4.1	1,120	3.8
Total respondents	66,887		86,006		88,544	

[a] This is a new category for 1995.
[b] Category is combined with Health (outpatient) in 1995.
[c] Category is combined with Residential facility in 1995.
[d] Category is combined with Health (inpatient) in 1995.
[e] Category is combined with "other" in 1995.

TABLE 4.16

Percentage of Working NASW Members, by Secondary Setting and Highest Degree, 1995

Setting	BSW	MSW	PhD–DSW
Business–industry[a]	0.3	0.1	0.2
Colleges–universities	5.1	6.9	21.9
Courts–justice system	6.1	1.6	1.1
Health (inpatient)[a]	8.5	7.4	5.0
Health (outpatient)[a]	10.7	12.7	6.5
Managed care[a]	0.2	0.2	0.1
Mental health (inpatient)[a]	0.2	0.3	0.2
Mental health (outpatient)[a]	1.1	1.8	0.8
Private group	7.2	12.5	11.1
Private solo	17.0	33.6	34.5
Residential facility[a]	23.4	7.0	3.8
School (preschool–grade 12)	6.9	2.8	1.5
Social services agency	18.2	9.5	9.1
Other[a]	7.4	3.7	4.3
Total respondents	625	26,759	1,809
Percent of total	2.1	91.7	6.2

Note: N = 29,193.

[a]These are new or combined former categories for 1995. It may take two or more years before these are accurate representations of the NASW membership.

Secondary Setting, by Gender

Gender differences for secondary practice settings were less pronounced than they were for primary settings. Not surprisingly, the proportion of NASW members with a secondary setting of private group or private solo practice is considerably higher than the proportion citing private group or solo practice as a primary setting, and gender distinctions also reverse from primary to secondary in this category. For example, 14.9 percent of female respondents in 1995 identified their primary setting of practice as private solo compared with 12.7 percent of male respondents. For secondary setting, the proportions reverse: Men constitute 34.2 percent of responding members with private solo as their secondary practice, compared with 32.5 percent of the women. Men also represent a higher proportion of members with private group practice as their secondary setting—14.0 percent compared with 11.6 percent of responding women.

A higher proportion of women worked in the secondary settings of residential facilities, inpatient health, schools, and social services agencies in 1995. Although the proportion of men in colleges and universities is higher for both primary and secondary settings, the difference is less significant in the secondary setting.

Secondary Setting, by Ethnicity

A higher proportion of Other Hispanic respondents listed membership organizations as their secondary setting, and a higher proportion of Puerto Rican respondents cited institutions. There was a higher ratio of Native American, Asian, and Other Hispanic respondents than respondents of other ethnic groups in hospitals and a higher proportion of Native American and African American respondents in clinics. A higher proportion of Native American, African American, Chicano, and Puerto Rican respondents than respondents of other ethnic groups cited the courts–justice system, and a higher proportion of Native American, Asian, and African American respondents listed colleges–universities.

The findings for secondary setting by ethnicity also differ from those for primary setting. A higher proportion of Other Hispanic members, white respondents, and members of mixed heritage identified both private group and private solo practice as their secondary setting of practice than respondents of other ethnic groups. Inpatient health facilities were identified by a higher proportion of Native American and Chicano members than by other ethnic groups, whereas outpatient health facilities were cited by a higher proportion of African American and Puerto Rican members. A higher proportion of African American and Chicano members than respondents of other ethnic groups identified social services agencies as their secondary setting. Native Americans, Asians, and members of mixed heritage were overrepresented in colleges–universities.

Secondary Setting, by Age

Trends in regard to secondary setting and age of NASW members are consistent with those found for primary settings. Colleges–universities and private solo practice are more frequently identified as secondary practice settings by members over age 40. On the other hand, those with a secondary practice in the courts–criminal justice system, social services agencies, residential facilities, inpatient and outpatient health facilities, and schools (preschool through grade 12) tend to be younger (21 to 35 years).

CHAPTER HIGHLIGHTS

- The not-for-profit sector was the auspice of practice for the largest proportion of NASW members.
- The second-ranked auspice was government at the combined local, state, federal, and military levels.
- By individual categories, the members identified their work auspice, in rank order, to be private not-for-profit, private for-profit, and public local.
- The proportion of members working under a government auspice and for not-for-profit organizations decreased.
- The proportion of members working under private for-profit auspices increased.
- The primary auspices differed on the basis of the highest social work degree held. The majority of BSWs cited government, followed by the private not-for-profit sector; the majority of MSWs cited private not-for-profit, followed by the private for-profit sector; the majority of PhD–DSWs cited the not-for-profit sector, followed by state government.
- The highest proportion of members working for the military was at the doctoral level.
- The less-experienced members worked in traditional social work agencies.
- A higher proportion of male members than female members reported their primary auspice as government.
- Members over the age of 40 more frequently worked in for-profit agencies than did younger members, whereas those under age 40 tended to work in not-for-profit agencies.
- Proportionately more male members than female members indicated private for-profit as their secondary auspice.
- A higher proportion of members of color were employed by the local, state, or federal government.
- Proportionately more white members than those of other ethnic groups reported the private for-profit sector as their primary and secondary auspices.
- African American members had the highest proportional representation in the military of any ethnic group.

- Members who worked under not-for-profit or military auspices were overrepresented in the functions of administration–management compared with those who worked under other auspices; those who worked in state government tended to be underrepresented in clinical practice.
- Approximately half the members who reported a secondary auspice identified it as the private for-profit sector.
- The second-ranked secondary auspice was the private not-for-profit sector, and the third-ranked was local government.
- The largest proportion of members who identified government at any level as their secondary auspice were at the BSW level.
- Social services agencies were ranked first as the primary setting of social work practice, followed by inpatient and outpatient health facilities.
- Private solo and private group practice, when combined, was the second-ranked primary setting of practice.
- The vast majority of PhD–DSW members were in private solo practice or worked in a college or university.
- Proportionately more BSWs worked in social services agencies, residential facilities, and the courts–justice system than did MSWs and PhD–DSWs.
- More recent graduates and those with less experience tended to work in social services agencies, inpatient and outpatient health facilities, and residential care facilities.
- Respondents who earned their highest degree at earlier dates and had more years of experience were disproportionately represented among members whose primary setting was private solo practice.
- Members entered private solo practice as a secondary setting much sooner after graduation than as a primary setting.
- Male members were disproportionately represented in the primary practice settings of colleges–universities and outpatient health and residential facilities.
- A higher proportion of members of color cited social services agencies as their primary setting.
- A higher proportion of white members were in the primary settings of solo and private group practice.
- Approximately 46 percent of those who indicated they had a secondary setting were in private individual or group practice, the same level as in 1991.
- The higher proportion of male members than of female members in private solo and group practice as a secondary setting reversed the proportions found for primary setting.

CHAPTER 5

WHAT WE DO

AREAS OF PRACTICE, PRACTICE FOCUS, AND FUNCTIONS PERFORMED

PRIMARY PRACTICE AREA

For all three study years, 1988, 1991, and 1995, the largest proportion of respondents were in the primary practice area of mental health. Of the 89,432 respondents to this question in 1995, 38.8 percent (34,715) cited mental health as their primary practice area compared with 35.4 percent in 1991 and 34.3 percent in 1988. (For 1995, the previous categories of mental health and mental and developmental disabilities were recoded into the one category of mental health.) The second-ranked practice area for the three years was children and families, with 24.9 percent (22,258) of the respondents in 1995, 27.6 percent in 1991, and 28.6 percent in 1988. (In 1991 and 1988, children and families were separate categories. In 1995, these categories were combined into the single category of children–families.) Medical health ranked third in 1995 and 1988, but the combination that now constitutes "other" was ranked third in 1991 (see Table 5.1).

The proportion of NASW members with a primary practice area of mental health continues to grow. At the same time, the proportion of members with a primary practice area of children and families has declined over the years. The proportion of members in the practice areas of aging, criminal justice, and occupational social work has remained consistent over time.

TABLE 5.1

Percentage of Working NASW Members, by Primary Practice Area

Primary Practice	1988	1991	1995
Children[a]	16.3	16.3	
Children–families[b]			24.9
Combined[c]	4.9	5.5	
Community organization–planning[c]	1.3	1.1	
Criminal justice	1.3	1.2	1.2
Elderly people	4.7	4.5	4.6
Family services[a]	12.3	11.3	
Group services[c]	0.5	0.5	
Medical health	13.2	12.5	13.0
Mental and developmental disabilities[d]	3.0	2.7	
Mental health[d]	31.3	32.7	
Mental health[b]			38.8
Occupational social work	0.8	0.8	0.8
Other disabilities[c]	0.5	0.5	
Public assistance[c]	0.9	0.8	
Schools	4.3	4.7	5.2
Substance abuse[c]	4.0	4.6	
Other (previous)[c]	0.8	0.2	
Other (1995)[b]			11.4
Total respondents	67,943	87,129	89,432

[a]These categories are combined into children–families in 1995.
[b]These are new categories in 1995.
[c]These categories are combined into "other" in 1995.
[d]These categories are combined into mental health in 1995.

Primary Focus

Of the 113,352 employed members of NASW in 1995, only 12,491 (11.0 percent) responded to the question about primary focus. This question was added to the revised demographic profile form in 1994. Of those responding, family issues and individual–behavior were cited most frequently as the primary focus, at 26.3 percent (3,284) and 23.1 percent (2,881), respectively. Health, at 14.7 percent (1,840), was ranked third as the primary focus of practice (see Table 5.2).

The primary focus of members is related to the primary auspice of practice. For example, members with a primary focus of alcohol–drugs tended to work in the private for-profit or private not-for-profit sector. Those with a primary focus of employment-related issues worked under private for-profit auspices proportionately more than under any other auspice of practice. The primary foci of violence and victims of crimes, health, grief–bereavement, and disabilities, however, were more often associated with the not-for-profit sector. The largest proportion of members with a primary focus of individual–behavior work in the private for-profit sector, probably in group or individual private practice. Of those members working in the military, a disproportionate number cited their primary focus as family issues and violence–victimization.

TABLE 5.2

Percentage of Working NASW Members, by Primary and Secondary Focus, 1995

Focus	Primary (%)	Secondary (%)
Alcohol–drugs	9.8	9.0
Disabilities	6.0	3.3
Employment	1.7	1.6
Family issues	26.3	26.7
Grief–bereavement	2.5	5.7
Health	14.7	8.0
Housing	0.6	0.5
Income maintenance	0.4	0.4
Individual–behavior	23.1	28.6
International	0.2	0.5
Violence–victimization	2.2	3.4
Other	12.6	12.1
Total respondents	12,491	4,054
Percent of total	75.5	24.5

Note: N = 16,545.

Primary Practice Area, by Highest Degree Held

There are some noteworthy distinctions in the members' primary practice area on the basis of their highest degrees. In 1995, proportionately more BSW respondents designated aging, children–families, and medical and mental health as their primary practice areas, and proportionately fewer cited schools, criminal justice, and occupational social work. Proportionately more PhD–DSW respondents listed mental health, children–families, and "other" as their primary practice areas, and proportionately fewer noted medical health, occupational social work, and aging.

The proportional differences in primary practice on the basis of highest degree may reflect a differential utilization pattern of personnel in human services agencies. It may also reflect the personal preferences of NASW members and different pay scales in various practice areas. As Table 5.3 shows, relatively few NASW members worked in criminal justice, occupational social work, and schools. This pattern is consistent with findings for 1988 and 1991.

Patterns related to secondary practice are similar to those of primary practice. The largest proportion of members with the MSW as their highest degree identified their secondary practice area as mental health or children and families. PhD–DSW members were concentrated in the secondary practice area of mental health, whereas BSW members were

TABLE 5.3

Percentage of Working NASW Members, by Primary Practice and Highest Degree, 1995

Primary Practice	BSW	MSW	PhD–DSW
Aging	16.7	4.2	3.7
Children–families	29.2	24.9	19.6
Criminal justice	2.5	1.1	1.1
Medical health	17.0	13.2	7.7
Mental health	18.3	39.6	40.7
Occupational social work	0.6	0.8	1.0
Schools	2.6	5.4	4.1
Other	13.2	10.8	22.2
Total respondents	3,261	81,801	3,840
Percent of total	3.7	92.0	4.3

Note: N = 88,902.

overrepresented in the secondary practice areas of aging, criminal justice, and medical health.

Primary Practice Area, by Date of Highest Social Work Degree

A few trends are discernible when primary practice area is analyzed in relation to the date of receipt of the highest social work degree. In the practice areas of aging, children and families, medical health, and "other," recent graduates (those who received their highest social work degree after 1985) were proportionately overrepresented, whereas in mental health they were proportionately underrepresented.

The primary practice areas of mental health and schools included a larger proportion of members who received their highest degree prior to 1981 than in other practice areas. Proportionately fewer members with an early degree date cited "other" as their primary practice area. More recent graduates may find employment in practice areas such as substance abuse, public assistance, and mental retardation–developmental disabilities, areas that fall under the other categories of practice.

Primary Focus, by Date of Highest Social Work Degree

There are a few areas of primary focus that are associated with a recent date of highest social work degree. For example, members who received their highest social work degree after 1980 are overrepresented in the primary focus areas of alcohol–drug abuse, grief–bereavement, and violence–victimization. In contrast, those with a primary focus of "other" tend to be concentrated among members with an earlier date of highest degree.

Primary Practice Area, by Years of Experience

When the experience of NASW members by primary practice area is examined, patterns emerge that are similar to those found for date of highest social work degree. Members whose primary practice areas were children and families, criminal justice, and aging reported less experience, and those in mental health, occupational social work, and schools reported more experience than did members in other primary practice areas.

There appears to be a shift away from the practice areas of children–families and aging between six and 10 years of experience. After five years, there is a noticeable increase in the proportion of NASW members in mental health practice (see Table 5.4). Members with a primary

TABLE 5.4

Percentage of Working NASW Members, by Primary Practice Area and
Years of Experience, 1995

Primary Practice Area	Less than 2	2–5	6–10	11–15	More than 16
		Years of Experience			
Aging	16.4	20.2	20.3	17.1	26.0
Children–families	16.6	19.2	19.6	17.4	27.3
Criminal justice	16.8	17.7	16.8	16.6	32.1
Medical health	12.7	17.4	20.6	20.1	29.1
Mental health	8.9	14.2	19.6	21.6	35.3
Occupational social work	12.3	12.7	22.6	22.6	29.8
Schools	9.4	14.1	19.5	21.6	35.4
Other	16.6	17.0	19.1	17.5	30.9
Total respondents	10,291	13,500	16,161	16,203	25,847
Percent of total	12.5	16.5	19.7	19.8	31.5

Note: N = 82,002.

practice area of medical health are well distributed among all experience levels.

Some alternative explanations can be derived from these findings.
First, the predominantly agency- and institution-based practice areas of
children and families, aging, and criminal justice may be more receptive
to hiring new and recent graduates than many other practice areas
because of the sheer number of practitioners needed. Second, the low
levels of pay may invite entry-level practitioners rather than more
experienced practitioners who have greater mobility and marketability
by virtue of their experience. After gaining experience in these primary
practice areas, NASW members are likely to move into other areas of
practice, making room for new graduates to assume these positions and
thus continue the cycle.

Primary Practice Area, by Gender

NASW members' selection of practice areas seems to reflect a gender-
based role distinction apparent in the population as a whole. Whether
for reasons of opportunity or preference, women frequently are the
primary caretakers of the family and children, elderly people, and those

who are sick. Information provided by NASW members in 1995 reflects these trends. Proportionately more female respondents worked in the primary practice areas of aging, children and family services, medical health, and schools. Male members were proportionately overrepresented in mental health, criminal justice, occupational social work, and "other" (see Table 5.5). These findings were the same in regard to secondary practice area.

Primary Focus, by Gender

Although only about 11 percent (12,427) of employed NASW members in 1995 responded to both the question about gender and that about primary focus, some interesting gender differences are apparent. Men identified alcohol and drugs or individual–behavior as the primary focus of their work proportionately more frequently than did women. On the other hand, women more often identified family issues, grief–bereavement, or health as the primary focus of their work (see Table 5.6).

TABLE 5.5

Percentage of NASW Members, by Primary and Secondary Practice Area and Gender, 1995

Practice Area	Primary		Secondary	
	Female	Male	Female	Male
Aging	86.0	14.0	80.8	19.2
Children–families	77.8	22.2	74.1	25.9
Criminal justice	61.2	38.8	59.2	40.8
Medical health	84.7	15.3	78.0	22.0
Mental health	74.4	25.6	70.4	29.6
Occupational social work	68.6	31.4	62.6	37.4
Schools	80.9	19.1	75.9	24.1
Other	71.1	28.9	70.8	29.2
Total respondents	67,669	20,328	27,415	10,390
Percent of total	76.9	23.1	72.5	27.5

Note: $N = 125,802$.

TABLE 5.6

Percentage of Working NASW Members, by Primary and Secondary Focus and Gender, 1995

Focus	Primary Focus		Secondary Focus	
	Female	Male	Female	Male
Alcohol–drugs	72.1	27.9	66.4	33.6
Disabilities	80.3	19.7	78.4	21.6
Employment	74.8	25.2	83.1	16.9
Family issues	81.2	18.8	75.7	24.3
Grief–bereavement	91.9	8.1	86.1	13.9
Health	83.7	16.3	78.5	21.5
Housing	72.7	27.3	59.1	40.9
Income maintenance	71.7	28.3	61.1	38.9
Individual–behavior	74.4	25.6	71.2	28.8
International	75.0	25.0	61.9	38.1
Violence–victims	82.9	17.1	73.0	27.0
Other	76.2	23.8	72.7	27.3
Total respondents	9,756	2,671	2,984	1,053
Percent of total	78.5	21.5	73.9	26.1

Note: Primary, N = 12,427; secondary, N = 4,037.

Primary Practice Area, by Ethnicity

There are some distinctive patterns when primary practice area is examined in relation to ethnicity. In 1995, the largest proportion of white, Asian, Chicano, Puerto Rican, and Other Hispanic members identified mental health as their primary practice area. Compared with other ethnic groups, a higher proportion of Native Americans, African Americans, and members of mixed heritage identified their primary practice area as children and families. Also compared with other ethnic groups, Asian members constitute a higher proportion of those with a primary practice area of aging. Similarly, the proportion of Chicanos with a primary practice area of children and families is higher than that for other ethnic groups, as is the proportion of Native American and Asian members in medical health. Schools included a higher proportion of African American and Puerto Rican members (see Table 5.7).

TABLE 5.7

Percentage of Working NASW Members, by Primary Practice Area and Ethnicity, 1995

Primary Practice Area	Ethnicity									Number of Respondents	Percentage in Practice Area
	Native American	Asian	African American	Chicano	Puerto Rican	Other Hispanic	White	Mixed Heritage	Other		
Aging	4.2	6.1	3.8	2.5	3.7	3.3	4.6	4.5	1.9	3,761	4.6
Children–families	31.3	27.9	32.4	33.0	25.0	30.6	24.2	28.2	21.2	20,476	24.9
Criminal justice	1.6	1.7	2.3	1.4	1.5	1.1	1.1	1.2	1.9	998	1.2
Medical health	16.5	16.7	13.7	12.7	12.3	12.3	13.0	12.4	17.3	10,728	13.1
Mental health	29.2	30.3	24.6	34.1	32.3	33.1	40.0	35.9	38.5	31,795	38.7
Occupational social work	0.2	1.0	0.8	0.6	0.5	1.0	0.8	0.5	1.9	679	0.8
Schools	4.2	5.4	9.3	5.3	10.4	6.9	4.9	5.9	7.7	4,301	5.2
Other	12.7	11.0	13.2	10.5	14.5	11.8	11.3	11.5	9.6	9,370	11.4
Total respondents	425	1,421	4,264	812	657	815	72,723	939	52	82,108	
Percent of total	0.5	1.7	5.2	1.0	0.8	1.0	88.6	1.1	0.1		100.0

Primary Focus, by Ethnicity

Of the 12,427 employed NASW members responding to both the questions about primary focus and ethnicity, there are some distinguishing characteristics. There is an overrepresentation of Puerto Rican members and an underrepresentation of Chicano members in the primary focus area of alcohol and drug abuse. There is also a higher proportion of Puerto Rican members who identified a primary focus of disabilities than those of other ethnic groups. Chicano and Other Hispanic members are overrepresented in the area of family issues, whereas Native American and African American members are overrepresented in health. A higher proportion of Native American and white members identified individual–behavior as their primary focus than those of other ethnic groups.

Primary Practice Area, by Age

The patterns that emerged in regard to primary practice area by age were similar to those reported in relation to primary practice by experience. The primary practice areas of children and families, aging, and medical health were likely to have a higher proportion of those age 40 or under than were other practice areas. Members age 41 or older were more likely to have a primary practice area of mental health or combined areas.

Primary Focus, by Age

Age is not a significant factor in differentiating the primary focus of members' practice. There is a slight tendency for younger members (under age 40) to identify developmental disabilities, grief–bereavement, health, and violence as their primary focus more frequently than members over the age of 40. Similarly, older members more frequently identify individual–behavior as the primary focus of their practice than do younger members.

SECONDARY PRACTICE AREA

In 1995, 33.9 percent (38,425) of the total data set of employed NASW members indicated that they had a secondary practice area, down from 37.0 percent in 1991. For all three study years, mental health, children and families, and "other" were ranked first through third, respectively, as secondary areas of practice (see Table 5.8).

TABLE 5.8

Percentage of Working NASW Members, by Secondary Practice Area

Secondary Practice Area	1988	1991	1995
Children–families	32.5	31.6	28.8
Criminal justice	1.4	1.3	1.5
Elderly people	6.1	5.3	5.4
Medical health	6.2	5.9	6.5
Mental health	29.4	29.8	32.5
Occupational social work	0.9	1.0	1.0
Schools	2.0	2.2	2.6
Other	21.6	23.0	21.6
Total respondents	27,703	37,153	38,425

There are several possible explanations for the relatively high proportion of NASW members who indicated a secondary practice area. First, professionals who are interested in more than one practice area may fulfill their occupational interests through part-time employment or consultation in a secondary setting.

Second, although members were asked to indicate their practice area by their primary and secondary places of employment, if any, some members may have responded to the question by indicating multiple areas of practice within their same (primary) employment setting. This possibility is enhanced by the number of social work practice settings (such as inpatient and outpatient mental health facilities, business and industry, social services agencies, and schools) that offer a variety of services to a broad base of clients.

Third, the mobility in the profession may allow social workers to develop expertise in one practice area and then move to a new primary practice area. In such instances, members may classify their original primary practice area as "secondary." Fourth, because of their relatively low primary incomes, many NASW members may find it necessary to engage in a secondary income-producing activity.

Secondary Practice Area, by Degree

Consistent with the findings about the primary practice area by degree, there are also discernible trends among employed NASW members with a secondary practice area on the basis of their highest degrees. In 1995, relatively few BSWs—190, or 19.4 percent—reported having a second-ary practice area in mental health, compared with MSWs at 32.7 percent (11,495) and PhD–DSWs at 34.8 percent (737). The proportion of BSWs with a secondary practice area of aging, criminal justice, medical health, or schools was higher than for MSWs and PhD–DSWs. Doctoral-level members reported a higher proportion of mental health, children and families, and other secondary practice areas (see Table 5.9).

Secondary Practice Area, by Ethnicity

Children and families, mental health, and "other" were identified as the largest categories of secondary practice by all ethnic groups. The largest proportion of Asian, African American, Chicano, and members of mixed heritage identified children and families as their secondary practice area. Mental health was identified as the largest secondary practice area for Puerto Rican, Other Hispanic, and white members.

Consistent with the findings regarding primary practice and ethnicity, mental health as a secondary practice area included a higher proportion of white members, and school social work included a higher proportion of African American and Other Hispanic members. The highest propor-tion of those with a secondary practice area of medical health were

TABLE 5.9

Percentage of Working NASW Members, by Secondary Practice Area and Highest Degree, 1995

Secondary Practice Area	BSW	MSW	PhD–DSW
Children–families	29.0	29.1	24.5
Criminal justice	2.6	1.5	1.5
Elderly people	12.9	5.3	4.6
Medical health	8.0	6.5	5.5
Mental health	19.4	32.7	34.8
Occupational social work	1.0	1.0	1.4
Schools	5.1	2.5	3.5
Other	22.1	21.4	24.3
Total respondents	979	35,106	2,118
Percent of total	2.6	91.9	5.5

Note: N = 38,203.

Chicano. Aging included a higher proportion of Asian, Other Hispanic, and members of mixed heritage.

Secondary Practice Area, by Date of Highest Social Work Degree

Consistent with the findings regarding primary practice areas in 1995, aging, children and families, and other secondary practice areas included a higher proportion of more recent graduates (1990 or later). Similarly, fewer recent graduates cited a secondary practice area of mental health than did earlier graduates.

Secondary Practice Area, by Years of Experience

Findings in regard to secondary practice by experience are consistent with those of primary practice by experience in most areas. However, whereas the less experienced members were overrepresented in the primary practice area of aging, the reverse is true in regard to secondary practice. Aging, as a secondary practice area, includes a disproportionate number of the most experienced members—those with more than 20 years of experience. Similarly, members with a primary practice area of schools were overrepresented among the more experienced members, but for schools as a secondary practice area the least experienced members were disproportionately represented.

Secondary Practice Area, by Age

Consistent with the findings regarding primary practice areas, a higher proportion of younger NASW members (age 40 or under) identified their secondary practice area as aging, children and families, medical health, or schools. A higher proportion of members over age 40 cited a secondary practice area of mental health.

PRIMARY FUNCTION

The overwhelming majority of respondents cited clinical–direct service as their primary function—70.0 percent (63,853) of the 91,226 members responding to this question in 1995. The proportion of NASW members with a primary function of clinical–direct service continues to grow. In 1991, 68.5 percent of respondents cited clinical–direct service as their primary function, up from 65.1 percent in 1988. The second-ranked category in all three study years was management, representing 15.5 percent (14,181) of respondents in 1995, down from 16.2 percent in 1991 and 17.7 percent in 1988 (see Table 5.10).

TABLE 5.10

Percentage of Working NASW Members, by Primary Function

Function	1988	1991	1995
Administration–management	17.7	16.2	15.5
Clinical–direct service	65.1	68.5	70.0
Community organizing–advocacy[a]			0.2
Policy	1.0	0.9	0.8
Research	0.4	0.4	0.5
Supervision	6.4	6.1	5.5
Teaching	4.5	4.2	4.1
Training[a]			0.1
Other	4.9	3.7	3.3
Total respondents	72,239	88,925	91,226

[a]These are new categories in 1995.

These data suggest a significant skewing between direct (micro) and indirect (macro) functions in social work practice that has increased over time. The combined functions of community organization, policy, and research represented only 1.5 percent (1,361) of the members in 1995. When management was factored in, the total for macro practice reached 17.0 percent (15,542). (Exact comparisons to prior years are not possible because of category changes on the demographic data collection form: the earlier form included categories of policy, research, planning, and consultation; the new form excludes planning and consultation but adds community organization.)

Relatively few NASW members have a primary function of supervision. This finding suggests that supervisors carry out multiple agency roles. The supervision function may be combined with clinical–direct service or with management.

Primary Function, by Highest Social Work Degree

When primary function is examined by highest social work degree held, some interesting findings emerge. In 1995, clinical–direct service was the primary function for the majority of BSW respondents (65.5 percent, or 2,218) and MSW respondents (71.7 percent, or 59,641). For PhD–DSWs, it was the primary function for 40.4 percent (1,652) of the

113

respondents. The second-highest proportion of doctoral-level members, 32.1 percent (1,311), identified teaching as their primary function. Across the three educational levels, those with PhD–DSWs were more likely to identify administration–management or research as their primary function than were BSWs or MSWs (see Table 5.11).

In 1995, a relatively consistent proportion of the respondents at the three educational levels identified management as their primary function: 16.7 percent (684) of the PhD–DSWs, 15.7 percent (13,033) of the MSWs, and 10.6 percent (359) of the BSWs. Although one would expect to find significantly more MSWs and PhD–DSWs in supervision, the findings suggest otherwise. A higher proportion of BSWs (4.6 percent, or 192) identified their primary function as supervision compared with 2.3 percent (96) of the PhD–DSWs. Community organization is largely the province of BSW-level members.

Primary Function, by Date of Highest Social Work Degree

When primary function is examined in relation to the date of receipt of the highest social work degree, several trends emerge. First, NASW members tend to assume the primary function of supervision after

TABLE 5.11

Percentage of Working NASW Members, by Primary Function and Highest Degree, 1995

Function	BSW	MSW	PhD–DSW
Administration–management	10.6	15.7	16.7
Clinical–direct service	65.5	71.7	40.4
Community organizing–advocacy	1.5	0.2	0.1
Policy	1.3	0.7	1.2
Research	0.3	0.3	3.7
Supervision	4.6	5.7	2.3
Teaching	5.7	2.7	32.1
Training	0.2	0.1	0.0
Other	10.4	3.0	3.4
Total respondents	3,387	83,209	4,090
Percent of total	3.7	91.8	4.5

Note: N = 90,686.

114

working in the field for several years. This pattern is even more pronounced for members with a primary function of administration–
management, most of whom received their highest degree before 1980
(see Table 5.12).

An unexpected finding was that the majority of respondents who
reported the primary function of research earned their highest degree
after 1985. This phenomenon may reflect the effects of changing
priorities in the human services, where demands for accountability may
have fostered a greater interest in research to demonstrate the effectiveness of practice. Also surprising is that the largest proportion of members who cited community organization–advocacy as their primary
function are the more recent graduates.

Primary Function, by Age

Findings related to primary function and age are consistent with those
of primary function and experience. The largest proportion of members
in management and teaching positions were over age 40, whereas the
heaviest concentration of members in clinical practice were under 40.
For example, of those between the ages of 26 and 30, 83.6 percent were
in clinical practice. Of those between the ages of 51 and 60, 18.7
percent were in management positions. Although only a very small
proportion of the NASW membership reported community organization as a primary function, those occupying such positions tended to be
younger. For example, of those in community organization, 20.8
percent (45) were between the ages of 26 and 30.

Primary Function, by Years of Experience

There are two significant observations about primary function in
relation to years of experience. First, a decided shift in function occurs
between two and five years of practice and between six and 10 years of
practice. The proportion of members engaged in the primary function
of community organization–advocacy dropped after five years of
experience. The proportion of NASW members who reported supervision as their primary function increased sharply at two to five years of
experience and again at six to 10 years of experience. Similarly, the
proportion of members who reported management as a primary
function increased at six to 10 years of experience and continued to
grow up to 20 years. The fact that members move rapidly into supervision should alert social work education programs to the continued

TABLE 5.12

Percentage of Working NASW Members, by Primary Function and Year of Highest Social Work Degree, 1995

Function	Before 1951	1951 -1960	1961 -1970	1971 -1975	1976 -1980	1981 -1985	1986 -1990	1990	Number of Respondents	Percentage in Function
					Year of Highest Degree					
Administration–management	0.2	2.5	17.0	16.6	21.4	17.5	13.7	11.0	13,521	15.4
Clinical–direct service	0.1	1.3	8.5	10.7	15.7	17.1	22.2	24.3	61,455	70.2
Community organizing–advocacy	0.0	2.3	4.1	5.0	7.2	9.0	18.6	53.9	221	0.3
Policy	0.0	1.3	11.0	16.4	16.2	12.3	15.6	27.2	691	0.8
Research	0.0	1.0	6.3	6.5	10.1	12.3	22.4	41.4	398	0.5
Supervision	0.3	1.9	11.2	14.0	19.8	19.4	18.6	14.7	4,828	5.5
Teaching	0.3	2.2	11.9	13.3	16.7	16.2	15.8	23.6	3,590	4.1
Training	0.0	0.0	3.1	12.5	17.2	17.2	25.0	25.0	64	0.1
Other	0.2	1.6	8.7	12.1	16.8	13.4	15.3	31.9	2,817	3.2
Total respondents	133	1,362	8,859	10,477	14,772	14,936	17,649	19,397	87,585	
Percent of total	0.2	1.6	10.1	12.0	16.9	17.1	20.2	22.1		100.0

importance of post-degree opportunities for professional development and the need to enhance the curriculum on supervision. Furthermore, schools need to develop continuing education–professional development programs in management and target them to members from their sixth to 10th year of practice (see Table 5.13).

Another significant observation is that a large proportion of the respondents in research and policy reported fewer than two years of experience. As with the observations related to the date of the highest degree, the political climate may have influenced the functions of NASW members. An alternative explanation may be that graduates enter practice aware of and eager to practice a full range of social work functions, but after about five years of practice, career mobility, opportunities, and more specialized areas of interest move them into functions other than research and planning.

Primary Function, by Gender

In 1995, a significantly higher proportion of female respondents reported their function as community organizing–advocacy, whereas a higher proportion of male respondents cited administration–management, teaching, or policy (see Table 5.14). However, the proportion of women in management positions has increased since 1988.

Primary Function, by Ethnicity

In 1995, a higher proportion of African American, Asian, and Puerto Rican members than those of other ethnic groups cited administration–management as their primary function. At the direct-service level, there was a smaller proportion of African Americans and a larger proportion of Other Hispanic and white members. Compared with other ethnic groups, a higher proportion of Native American and African American members identified their primary function as supervision (see Table 5.15).

Although only a small proportion of members reported their primary function as policy, a higher proportion of Native American, Asian, and African American members cited it. For teaching, there was a higher proportion of Asian and African American members. Of those in research, the proportion of Asian members is higher than among other ethnic groups.

Primary Function, by Primary Setting

Continuing the discussion begun in chapter 4, certain primary settings of practice are conducive to different levels of practice. For example, of

TABLE 5.13

Percentage of Working NASW Members in Each Primary Function, by Years of Experience, 1995

Function	Years of Experience							Number of Respondents	Percentage in Function
	Less than 2	2–5	6–10	11–15	16–20	21–25	More than 25		
Administration–management	4.3	8.3	16.7	22.5	20.3	15.3	12.7	12,961	15.7
Clinical–direct service	14.7	19.1	20.8	18.9	13.2	7.7	5.5	58,585	70.7
Community organizing–advocacy	25.0	28.5	12.3	12.7	7.5	4.8	9.2	228	.3
Policy	17.2	13.3	14.8	19.2	16.9	10.0	8.5	609	.7
Research	21.6	15.8	16.1	19.3	12.3	8.8	6.1	342	.4
Supervision	5.1	13.1	21.4	23.7	18.7	10.7	7.3	4,615	5.6
Teaching	10.3	7.9	13.5	18.2	19.7	14.3	16.1	3,228	3.9
Training	11.1	12.7	19.0	15.9	20.6	15.9	4.8	63	—
Other	22.4	12.5	16.6	19.5	13.7	8.5	6.8	2,213	2.7
Total respondents	10,502	13,617	16,301	16,312	12,368	7,746	5,998	82,844	
Percent of total	12.7	16.4	19.7	19.7	14.9	9.4	7.2		100.0

Note: Dash means percentage is so small as to be statistically insignificant.

TABLE 5.14

Percentage of Working NASW Members in Primary Function, by Gender

Function	1988 Female	1988 Male	1991 Female	1991 Male	1995 Female	1995 Male
Administration–management	55.7	44.3	60.0	40.0	63.8	36.2
Clinical–direct service	76.7	23.3	79.0	21.0	80.4	19.6
Community organizing–advocacy[a]					88.2	11.8
Policy	67.9	32.1	72.7	27.3	72.2	27.8
Research	70.2	29.8	71.3	28.7	73.6	26.4
Supervision	68.7	31.3	70.7	29.3	72.5	27.5
Teaching	60.5	39.5	65.9	34.1	70.2	29.8
Training[a]					79.7	20.3
Other	78.4	21.6	79.4	20.6	79.7	20.3
Total respondents	43,708	17,363	61,879	20,816	69,016	20,760
Percent of total	71.6	28.4	74.8	25.2	76.9	23.1

Note: For 1988, N = 61,071; for 1991, N = 82,695; and for 1995, N = 89,776.

[a]These are new categories in 1995.

TABLE 5.15

Percentage of Working NASW Members in Primary Function, by Ethnicity, 1995

Function	Native American	Asian	African American	Chicano	Puerto Rican	Other Hispanic	White	Mixed heritage	Other	Number of Respondents	Percentage in Function
Administration–management	15.6	18.3	20.8	13.8	20.6	13.0	15.0	15.7	24.5	12,927	15.4
Clinical–direct service	64.4	61.1	55.1	69.0	61.1	72.0	71.3	67.1	56.6	221	70.1
Community organizing–advocacy	0.5	0.8	0.3	0.2	0.0	0.2	0.3	0.1	1.9	58,721	0.3
Policy	1.4	1.6	1.2	0.5	0.5	0.8	0.8	0.8	0.0	668	0.8
Research	0.7	0.9	0.6	0.4	0.3	0.4	0.4	1.0	0.0	384	0.5
Supervision	9.4	6.2	9.6	5.5	8.1	5.1	5.2	7.5	1.9	4,621	5.5
Teaching	4.6	6.6	7.8	5.4	6.3	5.3	3.7	4.6	1.9	3,409	4.1
Training	0.0	0.1	0.0	0.1	0.3	0.1	0.1	0.0	0.0	63	0.1
Other	3.4	4.4	4.6	5.1	2.9	3.0	3.2	3.1	13.2	2,771	3.3
Total respondents	436	1,460	4,396	840	666	828	74,134	972	53	83,785	
Percent of total	0.5	1.7	5.2	1.0	0.8	1.0	88.5	1.2	0.1		100.0

those who identified the courts–justice system as their primary setting of practice, 19.7 percent (227) identified their primary function as administration, a proportion greater than for the working membership as a whole (see Table 4.13). Similarly, of those who identified social services agencies as their primary setting of practice, 26.8 percent (4,836) identified their primary function as administration and 24.5 percent (1,443) of those working in residential care settings identified their primary function as administration. In addition, a higher proportion of members who work in managed care, business and industry, and inpatient health facilities are in administrative positions than is true of the working membership as a whole.

Policy as a primary function is more frequently carried out in social services agencies and in the courts–criminal justice system than in other practice settings, and supervision is more frequently carried out by NASW members in the courts–justice system, residential facilities, and social services agencies. However, a smaller proportion (55.5 percent) of NASW members who identified social services agencies as their primary setting of practice are in clinical practice than is true for the working membership as a whole. Of those who cited social services agencies as their primary setting of practice, 26.8 percent are in administrative positions compared with 15.6 percent of the total working membership.

SECONDARY FUNCTION

Approximately 39 percent (43,649) of the 1995 data set of employed social workers reported a secondary function, equal to the proportion reporting a secondary function in 1988 but down significantly from 48.0 percent in 1991. Although the question pertaining to the secondary function refers to the function, if any, performed in a secondary job, the respondents may have reported a secondary function in their primary job that they considered to be of equal weight. Therefore, caution must be applied when interpreting these data because it is not known whether responses relate to a primary function in a secondary setting or a secondary function in a primary setting.

For the three study years, clinical–direct service was the most frequently cited primary function in a secondary job, at 35.9 percent in 1995, up from 32.8 percent in 1991 and 33.3 percent in 1988. Supervision ranked second, at 18.3 percent in 1995, 19.5 percent in 1991, and 18.4 percent in 1988 (see Table 5.16). Thus, a higher proportion of

TABLE 5.16

Percentage of NASW Members by Primary Function in a Secondary Job

Function	1988	1991	1995
Administration–management	10.1	10.0	9.8
Clinical–direct service	33.3	32.8	35.9
Community organizing–advocacy[a]			0.3
Policy	4.6	4.3	3.8
Research	1.9	1.9	1.9
Supervision	18.4	19.5	18.3
Teaching	14.7	15.2	15.1
Training[a]			0.2
Other	17.0	16.2	14.7
Total respondents	33,745	43,205	43,649

[a]These are new categories in 1995.

NASW members carry out supervision as a primary function in a secondary job than as a primary function in a primary job.

The finding that 15.1 percent (6,609) of the respondents in 1995 (compared with 15.2 percent in 1991 and 14.7 percent in 1988) reported teaching as their primary function in a second job suggests that a significantly higher proportion of members work as educators in secondary rather than primary jobs. Only 4.1 percent (3,748) of 1995 respondents, compared with 4.2 percent in 1991 and 4.5 percent in 1988, identified teaching as their primary function (see Table 5.10). These part-time educators may be associated with social work education programs as adjunct faculty or field instructors. Comparisons reveal a high degree of consistency between the primary and secondary functions.

The high proportion of respondents listing "other" as the secondary function may reflect the change in categories instituted in 1994. In both 1988 and 1991, 14.4 percent of members who indicated a secondary function listed consultation. With the elimination of this category from the new demographic form, those in consultation roles would likely indicate their secondary function as "other."

Secondary Function, by Highest Degree Held

When secondary function is examined in relation to the highest degree held by NASW members, some surprising findings emerge. Of the approximately 10 percent (4,245) of the respondents who cited management as a secondary function in 1995, 7.7 percent (208) were PhD–DSWs, 9.9 percent (3,904) were MSWs, and an unexpected 12.4 percent (133) were BSWs. It is also surprising that the largest proportion of members who cited policy and community organization as their secondary function were BSWs. Again, it is possible that some respondents indicated these functions as secondary functions in a primary job, whereas others indicated them as primary functions in a secondary job (see Table 5.17).

More in line with conventional wisdom is the finding that the majority of those who cited research as a secondary function were at the doctoral level. Another expected finding was that the largest proportion of members in all three educational levels listed clinical–direct service as their secondary function. However, the relative lack of PhD–DSWs in policy or community organization was not expected.

Several of the patterns found in regard to date of highest social work degree and primary function are reversed when date of highest social work degree is examined in relation to secondary function. For example, the largest proportion of those who cited teaching as a primary function received their degree before 1975. However, of those who cited teaching as a secondary function, the largest proportion received their

TABLE 5.17

Percentage of Working NASW Members, by Secondary Function and Highest Degree, 1995

Function	BSW	MSW	PhD–DSW
Administration–management	12.4	9.9	7.7
Clinical–direct service	25.5	36.5	30.6
Community organizing–advocacy	1.8	0.2	0.3
Policy	7.9	3.7	3.4
Research	2.2	1.2	12.7
Supervision	15.0	18.9	10.5
Teaching	17.9	14.9	18.5
Training	0.4	0.2	0.3
Other	16.9	14.5	15.9
Total respondents	1,070	39,613	2,691
Percent of total	2.5	91.3	6.2

Note: N = 43,374.

highest degree after 1980. The association between an earlier date of highest degree and the secondary function of supervision is much stronger than is the case for supervision as a primary function. The association between an earlier date of highest degree and the secondary function of supervision is even more pronounced than for date of highest degree and primary function. The largest proportion of members who cited research as a secondary function received their highest degree in recent years; this finding is consistent with that of research as a primary function.

Secondary Function, by Age

When secondary function is examined in relation to age, a different pattern emerges from that of primary function and age. Secondary functions may be used as a bridge between one level of practice and another. For example, a higher proportion of NASW members between the ages of 21 and 40 identified management, teaching, and policy as their secondary function than did those over age 40, the reverse of the pattern found for primary function or for secondary function in relation to experience. Those citing supervision as their secondary function tended to be in the middle to upper age ranges. For example, of the members identifying supervision as their secondary function, 26.7 percent were between the ages of 51 and 60.

Secondary Function, by Ethnicity

The findings regarding secondary function by ethnicity sometimes overlap with, but are by no means identical to, those regarding primary functions. As expected, the proportion of all ethnic groups with a secondary function of direct service was high. A lower proportion of Asian members, however, cited this function. On the other hand, the proportion of Asian members who identified research or community organization as their secondary function was higher than among other ethnic groups.

The proportion of Asian, African American, Chicano, and Other Hispanic members with management as a secondary function was higher than for those of other ethnic groups. Although policy ranked relatively low as a secondary function for all ethnic groups, the proportion of Native American and Asian members in this function was higher than for other ethnic groups.

The proportion of Asian, Puerto Rican, and white members with a secondary function of supervision was significantly higher than for other ethnic groups, and the proportion of Native American, Puerto Rican, and members of mixed heritage with a secondary function of teaching was higher than for other groups.

Despite the significant differences in primary and secondary functions by ethnicity, there is no clear explanatory variable. The lack of consistency between the primary and secondary functions by ethnicity suggests that the patterns are illusive.

Secondary Function, by Experience

There are less significant differences by experience in relation to secondary function than in relation to primary function. A higher proportion of less experienced members cited administration–management and teaching as secondary functions than as primary functions in these areas. The proportion of members engaged in supervision as a secondary function across all experience levels is significantly higher than as a primary function. Research, policy, and community organization–advocacy, consistent with findings for primary function, are over-represented among the less experienced members.

CHAPTER HIGHLIGHTS

- The primary practice area of the highest proportion of NASW members was mental health, followed by children–families and medical health.
- The proportion of members citing mental health as their primary practice area has risen consistently since 1988.
- A higher proportion of BSW members than MSW or PhD–DSW members reported aging, criminal justice, and medical health as their primary practice areas.
- A higher proportion of doctoral-level members than BSW or MSW members were in the primary practice areas of mental health, occupational social work, and "other."
- Among those who received their highest degree in earlier years, a higher proportion reported mental health and schools as their primary practice areas than did the more recent graduates.
- After five years of experience, the proportion of members who cited mental health as their primary practice area rose significantly.
- Those who received their highest degree relatively recently cited aging, children and families, medical health, and "other" as their primary practice areas.

- Proportionately more female members reported the primary practice areas of aging, children and families, medical health, and schools.
- Among the distinctions in primary and secondary practice areas on the basis of ethnicity, a higher proportion of white members than those of other ethnic groups were in mental health practice.
- Older members were concentrated in the practice areas of mental health or combined areas.
- A larger proportion of men identified alcohol–drugs and individual–behavior as their primary foci of practice.
- Approximately 34 percent of the employed NASW members had a secondary practice area, down from about 37 percent in 1991.
- Among the secondary practice areas, mental health, children and families, and "other" were ranked the highest.
- Within secondary practice areas, MSWs and PhD–DSWs were disproportionately represented in mental health, and BSWs were overrepresented in aging, criminal justice, and medical health.
- The overwhelming majority of members reported their primary function as clinical–direct service, and direct service was the modal response for BSW, MSW, and doctoral-level members.
- The second-ranked primary function was management.
- Since 1988, there has been a downward trend in the proportion of members in macro-level practice.
- Community organization, policy, and research combined was the primary function of only 1.5 percent of the members.
- A significantly higher proportion of female members cited their primary function as clinical–direct service.
- BSW members were more likely than MSW and PhD–DSW members to identify community organization as their primary function.
- The proportion of members at the three educational levels who identified management as their primary function was relatively consistent.
- The career path of NASW members appears to follow a predictable and sequenced pattern of clinical–direct service, supervision, and management.
- Approximately 39 percent of members reported a secondary function, a significant decrease from 48.0 percent in 1991 but consistent with the 39.0 percent reported in 1988.

- Clinical–direct service was the most frequently identified secondary function, followed by supervision.
- A higher proportion of members cited macro-level practice as a secondary function than as a primary function.

CHAPTER 6

WHAT WE EARN

INCOME OF NASW MEMBERS

This chapter presents information about the salaries that NASW members earned in 1995 with comparisons to 1991 and 1988. Only members who were working full-time in the three study years are included in this analysis of income. Part-time workers are excluded because they were likely to earn lower salaries by virtue of their part-time status and thus negatively affect aggregate incomes.

In 1993, NASW conducted a sample survey of its membership to update information on salaries (Gibelman & Schervish, 1993a). The sample comprised two distinct groups: (1) those with two years of experience or less (approximately 50 percent of the sample) and (2) those randomly selected from the full membership who were employed full-time. The survey was mailed to 7,300 members in April 1993, and the response rate was 42.8 percent (3,121). Because the data from this sample study include a disproportionate number of people with relatively few years of experience, the findings may be skewed in a downward direction. However, the studies for the 1988 and 1991 membership years had revealed that salaries tend to rise more quickly during the first five years of practice. Thus, the major changes in salary are likely to be evident for those at the lower experience levels (Gibelman & Schervish, 1993a, 1993b). With these caveats in mind, data from the 1993 sample survey are also included, as appropriate.

A large proportion of members did not respond to the question about their salaries. In 1995, 42,230 members (37.3 percent of the data set of 113,352) reported their salaries from full-time employment, down from 40.9 percent in 1991 but up considerably from 11.6 percent of the data set in 1988.

NASW RECOMMENDED SALARIES

In June 1990, the NASW Board of Directors adopted the following recommended minimum annual salaries for social workers: BSW, $20,000; MSW, $25,000; ACSW or MSW plus two years of social work experience, $30,000; and advanced professional (MSW plus special expertise at the administrative level), $45,000. NASW suggested that adjustments be considered for the economic conditions of specific geographic areas.

We can extrapolate from the 1990 figures using the BLS (1996a) Consumer Price Index-U deflator for 1990 (130.7) and 1995 (152.4). According to these figures, the 1995 equivalent of the 1990 recommendations would be BSW, $23,320; MSW, $29,150; ACSW or MSW plus two years of social work experience, $34,980; and advanced professional, $52,471. These standards may be compared with the actual salaries reported by NASW members in the three study years.

PRIMARY INCOME

For all study years, the responses were slightly positively skewed (0.55 for 1988, 0.39 for 1991, and 0.43 for 1995), with the majority of respondents falling midway between low salaries (defined for the purposes of this discussion as below $20,000) and high salaries ($50,000 or more). The respondents' median income was $34,215 in 1995, $31,264 in 1991, and $29,409 in 1988 (see Figure 6.1).

In 1995, 31.3 percent (13,255) of the respondents earned less than $30,000, down considerably from 44.4 percent in 1991 and 52.7 percent in 1988. Also in 1995, 46.6 percent (19,653) of respondents earned $35,000 or more compared with 33.3 percent in 1991 and 24.1 percent in 1988 (see Table 6.1).

At the upper end of the income scale, there was a modest gain between 1991 and 1995. In 1995, 32.0 percent (12,779) of the respondents reported salaries of $40,000 or more compared with 21.1 percent in 1991 and 14.6 percent in 1988. In 1995, 8.5 percent (3,577) of responding members reported salaries of $60,000 or more, whereas in 1991 and 1988, respectively, 3.4 percent and 2.6 percent of responding members reported salaries of $60,000 or more.

At the lower income levels, 4.8 percent (2,057) of responding 1995 members reported their salaries to be under $20,000 versus 8.0 percent in 1991 and 11.3 percent in 1988. The proportion of members reporting the lowest incomes has remained relatively consistent over the three

FIGURE 6.1

Distribution of Primary Income of NASW Members

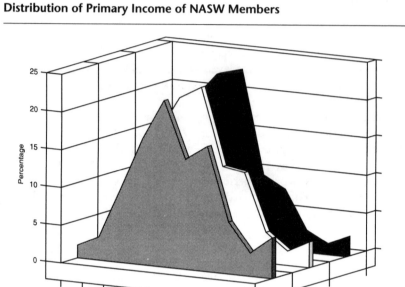

Income (in thousands of dollars)

study years. In 1995, 1.7 percent (733) of respondents reported salaries of under $15,000 compared with 2.1 percent in 1991 and 2.3 percent in 1988.

Contrast these salaries with those reported in NASW's 1961 salary study (Becker, 1961). MSW graduates in the class of 1960 earned a median salary of $5,500. However, as calculated by an inflator factor of 5.15 (the Consumer Price Index-U for 1961 = 29.9 and for 1995 = 152.4), the 1995 dollar value of those salaries is $28,325. Thus, although the current dollar value of income reported by NASW members has continued to increase, when converted to constant dollars (1982 = 100), the real income reported rose slightly between 1961 and 1988, declined between 1988 and 1991, then reached a plateau between 1991 and 1995 (see Figure 6.2).

TABLE 6.1

Percentage of NASW Members Working Full-Time, by Primary Income

Primary income	1988	1991	1995
Less than $15,000	2.3	2.1	1.7
$15,000–19,499	9.0	5.9	3.1
$20,000–24,999	19.0	15.7	9.8
$25,000–29,999	22.4	20.7	16.7
$30,000–34,999	23.2	22.4	22.1
$35,000–39,999	9.5	12.2	14.6
$40,000–49,999	7.9	11.7	16.6
$50,000–59,999	2.8	4.1	6.9
$60,000–69,999	1.3	1.9	3.1
$70,000 or more	2.6	3.4	5.4
Total respondents	10,023	41,300	42,230

The relatively modest rate of growth in salaries among NASW members from 1988 to 1991 and from 1991 to 1995, however, was consistent with wider socioeconomic trends. The Economic Policy Institute ("Declining Wages," 1992) reported that 80 percent of the U.S. workforce—including college graduates, white-collar workers, and most women—experienced substantial pay losses from 1987 to 1992, regardless of education.

Still, as BLS (1996b) data show, professional and technical workers in general received higher salaries than did NASW members in 1995. The salaries of NASW members grew at a slower rate than inflation (see Figure 6.3).

Primary Income, by Highest Social Work Degree and Year of Degree

As expected, NASW members with advanced degrees earned higher salaries. In the 1995 data set, the largest proportion of BSW respondents—46.4 percent (723)—earned $20,000 to $29,999; the largest proportion of MSW respondents—38.0 percent (14,696)—earned $30,000 to $39,999; and the largest proportion of PhD–DSW respondents—64.7 percent (1,158)—earned $40,000 or more (see Table 6.2). The income differentials by degree are most clearly evident at the upper and lower ranges. For example, 10.0 percent (86) of the BSW

131

FIGURE 6.2

Median Income of NASW Members in Current versus Constant (1982) Dollars

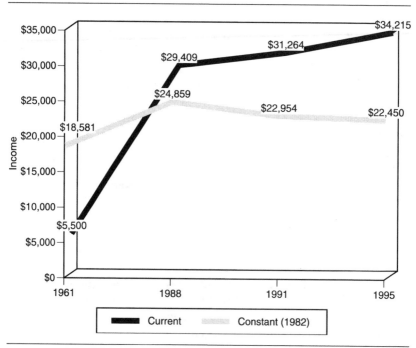

respondents earned less than $15,000 compared with 1.4 percent (559) of the MSW respondents and 1.0 percent (18) of the PhD–DSW respondents. At the other end of the income continuum, only 6.8 percent (105) of the BSW respondents versus 31.5 percent (12,166) of the MSW respondents and 64.7 percent (1,158) of the PhD–DSW respondents earned $40,000 or more.

As expected, the salaries were also positively associated with the year of receipt of the highest social work degree; that is, those who obtained their degree earlier earned higher salaries. For example, of those who earned $60,000 to $69,000 in 1995, 48.6 percent (614) received their degree before 1975 and 22.6 percent (286) received it between 1976 and 1980. On the other hand, less than 2 percent (145) of those who earned their highest degree after 1980 earned more than

FIGURE 6.3

Salaries of NASW Members versus Salaries in Other BLS Categories

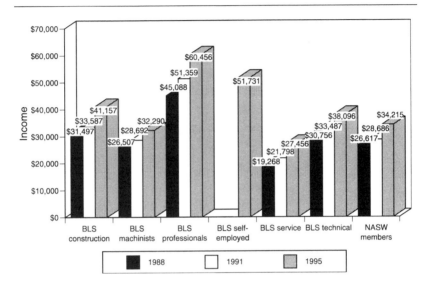

$60,000 in 1995. At the lower income levels, only 0.8 percent (4) of those who received their highest degree between 1951 and 1960 earned under $15,000 compared with 4.3 percent (397) of those who earned their degree after 1990.

The rate of increase appears to be more substantial for the first few years following graduation than for subsequent years. As Table 6.3 shows, salaries tend to rise more quickly during the first five years of practice. To achieve the same income growth experienced during the first five years of practice takes another 10 years. Income seems to level off after about 15 years after graduation; thereafter, there is relatively little difference in income related to the number of years out of school.

Primary Income, by Experience

Primary income is also positively correlated with years of experience; that is, the more experienced NASW members earn higher salaries. Of those earning less than $15,000 in 1995, 41.2 percent (258) had less than two years of experience and 5.3 percent (33) had 26 or more years of experience. Of the respondents with fewer than two years of experience, 28.9

133

TABLE 6.2

Percentage of NASW Members, by Primary Income and Highest Social Work Degree, 1995

Primary Income	BSW	MSW	PhD–DSW
Less than $15,000	10.0	1.4	1.0
$15,000–19,999	20.1	2.6	0.4
$20,000–29,999	46.4	26.6	8.3
$30,000–39,999	16.6	38.0	25.5
$40,000 or more	6.8	31.5	64.7
Total respondents	1,556	38,698	1,789
Percent of total	3.7	92.0	4.3

percent (1,452) earned $25,000 to $29,999 (the median range) compared with 18.6 percent (1,563) of those with six to 10 years of experience, and only 2.4 percent (53) of those earning $70,000 or more had two to five years of experience compared with 23.5 percent (523) who had 16 to 20 years of experience.

Unlike the incomes reviewed by year of receipt of the highest degree, an analysis of the relationship between years of experience and primary income reveals a delay in the growth of incomes for NASW members for the first five years. Between six and 20 years of experience, income appears to increase at about $1,000 per year until an apparent stagnation in income after about 20 years (see Table 6.4). This pattern may

TABLE 6.3

Income of NASW Members, by Year of Highest Social Work Degree, 1995

Year	Median	Mode	Midrange
1951–1960	$45,000–49,999	$45,000–49,999	$35,000–49,999
1961–1970	45,000–49,000	45,000–49,000	35,000–64,999
1971–1975	45,000–49,000	45,000–49,000	35,000–54,999
1976–1980	35,000–39,999	45,000–49,999	30,000–49,999
1981–1985	35,000–39,999	30,000–34,999	30,000–54,999
1986–1990	30,000–34,999	30,000–34,999	25,000–39,999
After 1990	25,000–29,999	25,000–29,999	20,000–34,999

Note: The midrange is achieved by excluding the highest 25 percent and the lowest 25 percent of reported salaries earned.

TABLE 6.4

Primary Income of NASW Members, by Years of Experience, 1995

Experience	Median	Mode	Midrange
Less than 2 years	$25,000–29,999	$25,000–29,999	$25,000–29,999
2–5 years	25,000–29,999	30,000–34,999	25,000–34,999
6–10 years	30,000–34,999	30,000–34,999	30,000–39,999
11–15 years	35,000–39,999	30,000–34,999	34,999–49,999
16–20 years	40,000–44,999	45,000–49,000	34,999–49,999
21–25 years	45,000–49,999	45,000–49,999	34,999–54,999
More than 26 years	45,000–49,999	45,000–49,999	40,000–54,999

Note: The midrange is achieved by excluding the highest 25 percent and the lowest 25 percent of reported salaries earned.

signal a reversal of patterns found in previous NASW salary studies (Becker, 1961; "Membership Survey," 1983; NASW, 1987), which reported an earlier plateau.

Primary Income, by Gender

The median income of NASW members in 1995 was $34,215. At the median, there was virtually the same proportion of male—14.3 percent (1,494)—and female—14.7 percent (4,573)—respondents. This quick look hides the significant gender-based difference in income for NASW members. When gender is controlled, the median income of the female respondents was $34,135 for women and $37,503 for men.

As Table 6.5 indicates, the income range of proportionately more female respondents was below the median, and the income range of a higher proportion of the male respondents was above the median. This differential is accentuated by the fact that the NASW membership is overwhelmingly female.

These findings are consistent with other studies of gender-related differences in the income of social workers (see Belon & Gould, 1977; Fanshel, 1976; Fortune & Hanks, 1988; Gibelman & Schervish, 1993a, 1995; Gould & Bok-Lim, 1976; Jennings & Daley, 1979; Landers, 1992; Scotch, 1971; Sowers-Hoag & Harrison, 1991; Strobino & McCoy, 1992; Sutton, 1982; Yamatani, 1982; York, 1987). Gibelman and Schervish (1993a) reported that men earned, on average, about

TABLE 6.5

Primary Income of NASW Members, by Gender, 1995

Primary Income	Female		Male		Total Respondents	
	n	%	*n*	%	*n*	%
Less than $15,000	582	1.9	143	1.4	725	1.7
$15,000–19,999	1,132	3.6	186	1.8	1,318	3.2
$20,000–29,999	9,166	29.5	1,919	18.4	11,085	26.6
$30,000–39,999	11,768	37.8	3,475	33.3	15,243	36.7
$40,000–49,999	4,759	15.3	2,105	20.1	6,864	16.5
$50,000–59,999	1,793	5.8	1,078	10.3	2,871	6.9
More than $60,000	1,971	6.3	1,536	14.7	3,507	8.4
Total respondents	31,171	74.9	10,442	25.1	41,613	100.0

5 percent more than women earned. When controlling for gender, the median income in 1993 for women was found to be $30,000 versus $34,000 for men.

Various explanations have been offered for the inequities in the incomes of male and female social workers. One view is that men disproportionately hold administrative–management positions that pay higher salaries; empirical support for this review is shown in chapter 5. It is also believed that men assume administrative positions earlier in their careers than do women and so earn higher salaries on the basis of the date of the degrees and years of experience (Belon & Gould, 1977; Jennings & Daley, 1979). However, both of these hypotheses were refuted by more detailed analysis (Gibelman & Schervish, 1995). Whatever the reason, the fact remains that male members earn significantly higher salaries than do female members.

Primary Income, by Ethnicity

Few differences were found in the primary income of NASW members by ethnicity, and those that were found were not statistically significant. There was a slight tendency for Native American, Chicano, Puerto Rican, and Other Hispanic members to earn lower salaries than members of other ethnic groups; for example, in 1995, 3.0 percent (11) of Puerto Rican respondents earned less than $15,000 compared with

1.5 percent (37) of the African American respondents and 1.8 percent (610) of white respondents. A narrower midrange appears for African American respondents than for other ethnic groups (see Table 6.6).

At the highest income level ($70,000 or more), white, mixed heritage, and other respondents were disproportionately represented (see Figure 6.4). For example, 5.5 percent (1,877) of white respondents, 6.5 percent (29) of mixed heritage respondents, and 18.8 percent (three) of other respondents earned $70,000 or more in contrast to 3.4 percent (84) of African American respondents and 2.3 percent (10) of Other Hispanic respondents. There was some variation by ethnicity within all the income ranges, but no consistent pattern.

Gibelman and Schervish (1993a) revealed that Other Hispanic members reported the highest mean salary, followed closely by Chicano, Puerto Rican, and African American members. In 1993, Native American and white respondents had the lowest mean salary of any ethnic group. For 1991 Gibelman and Schervish (1993b) found that those in the "other" category had a slightly higher mean income ($29,843), followed by Asian respondents ($29,431), white respondents ($28,424), and Puerto Rican respondents ($28,344). These patterns were repeated in 1995 when those in the "other" category had a significantly higher mean income ($46,093), followed by Asian ($39,436), mixed heritage ($38,760), Puerto Rican ($38,533), and African American respondents ($37,651) (see Table 6.6).

Primary Income, by Primary Practice Area

An analysis of the 1995 primary income by primary practice area shows that the median and mean salaries of the respondents fell within a narrow range: $32,499 to $40,472. However, there was a discernible trend in this midrange income by primary areas of practice. As Table 6.7 indicates, the midrange incomes of three basic groups of primary practice areas differed. Those with primary practice areas in services to elderly people and children–families earned $33,158 to $34,865 at the mean, with a midrange of $32,499 to $37,499. The mean income of respondents whose primary practice areas were criminal justice and medical health was $36,963 and $36,340, respectively, with a mean range of $32,499 to $47,499.

The highest income-producing areas of social work practice appear to be mental health, schools, and occupational social work. The mean for this group ranged from $38,781 to $40,472, with a midrange from $37,499 to $47,499. However, except for mental health services, these

TABLE 6.6

Primary Income of NASW Members, by Ethnicity, 1995

Ethnicity	n	Percentage of total	Annual Primary Income			
			25th Percentile	Median	Mean	75th Percentile
African American	2,487	6.4	$27,499	$37,499	$37,651	$32,499
Asian	724	1.9	32,499	37,499	39,436	47,499
Chicano	422	1.1	27,499	32,499	37,120	47,499
Mixed heritage	444	1.1	27,499	37,499	38,760	47,499
Native American	222	0.6	27,499	32,499	35,889	47,499
Other Hispanic	429	1.1	27,499	32,499	36,211	47,499
Puerto Rican	370	0.9	27,499	37,499	38,533	47,499
White	33,946	86.9	27,499	32,499	37,180	47,499
Other	16	0.0	37,499	42,499	46,093	52,499

Note: N = 39,060.

FIGURE 6.4

Percentage of NASW Members Reporting High and Low Earnings, by
Ethnicity, 1995

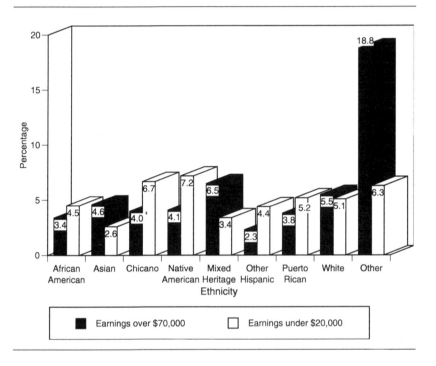

primary practice areas represent less than 7 percent of the respondents
who were working full-time.

As Figure 6.5 illustrates, NASW members reporting the highest
incomes ($70,000 or more) were concentrated in three primary practice
areas: mental health (9.3 percent), occupational social work (5.8
percent), and "other" (5.3 percent). In contrast, those reporting the
lowest incomes (under $15,000) were concentrated in occupational
social work (2.9 percent), "other" (2.3 percent), aging (2.1 percent),
and children–families (2.1 percent).

Primary Income, by Primary Setting

The midrange incomes for 1995 fell into five categories, according to
the primary settings in which the respondents practiced (see Table 6.8).

139

TABLE 6.7

Primary Income of NASW Members, by Primary Practice Area, 1995

Area	n	Percentage of Total	Annual Primary Income			
			25th Percentile	Median	Mean	75th Percentile
Aging	1,824	4.4	$27,499	$32,499	$33,158	$37,499
Children–families	10,430	25.3	27,499	32,499	34,865	37,499
Criminal justice	555	1.3	27,499	32,499	36,963	47,499
Medical health	5,704	13.9	27,499	32,499	36,340	42,499
Mental health	15,087	36.7	27,499	37,499	39,626	47,499
Occupational social work	312	0.8	32,499	37,499	40,472	47,499
Schools	2,381	5.8	32,499	37,499	38,781	47,499
Other	4,864	11.8	27,499	32,499	37,707	47,499

Note: N = 41,157.

FIGURE 6.5

Percentage of NASW Members Reporting High and Low Income, by Primary Practice Area, 1995

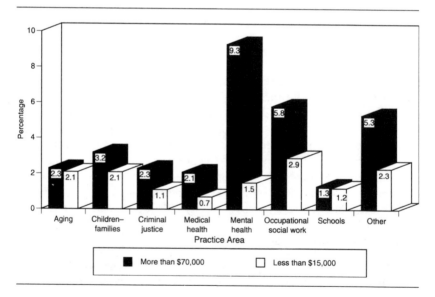

TABLE 6.8

Primary Income of NASW Members, by Primary Setting, 1995

Setting	n	Percentage of Total	25th Percentile	Median	Mean	75th Percentile
Business–industry	53	0.1	32,499	37,499	41,273	52,499
Colleges–universities	1,577	3.8	32,499	37,499	41,757	47,499
Courts–justice system	629	1.5	27,499	32,499	36,366	47,499
Health (inpatient)	8,251	20.1	27,499	32,499	36,011	42,499
Health (outpatient)	7,115	17.4	27,499	32,499	34,340	37,499
Managed care	88	0.2	32,499	37,499	39,601	42,499
Mental health (inpatient)	297	0.7	32,499	37,499	38,804	42,499
Mental health (outpatient)	925	2.3	27,499	37,499	38,283	47,499
Private group	1,591	3.9	32,499	47,499	45,164	52,499
Private solo	4,099	10.0	32,499	52,499	49,739	62,499
Residential	3,104	7.6	$22,499	$32,499	$32,546	$37,499
School (preschool– grade 12)	3,024	7.4	27,499	37,499	38,490	47,499
Social services agency	9,014	22.0	27,499	32,499	34,069	37,499
Other	1,205	2.9	27,499	37,499	39,785	47,499

Note: N = 40,972.

The low midrange category ($22,499 to $37,499, with a median of $32,499) consisted of respondents employed in residential facilities, social services agencies, and outpatient health. One explanation for the low income in these settings is that the workers tend to be newer graduates with less advanced degrees (BSWs rather than MSWs) than those in other settings.

The respondents in the second midrange category ($27,499 to $47,499) were employed in inpatient health (mean = $36,011), courts and justice system (mean = $36,366), outpatient mental health (mean = $38,283), schools (mean = $38,490), and "other" (mean = $39,785). The third category ($32,499 to $42,499) comprised

141

respondents who worked in managed care (mean = $39,601) and inpatient mental health (mean = $38,804). The median primary income for this category ($37,499) was above the median and mean for the total membership in 1995.

The fourth category ($32,499 to $47,499) consisted of respondents who were employed in colleges and universities. The fifth category ($32,499 to $62,499) comprised respondents who were in private practice—both private group and private solo as well as business–industry. The median and mean incomes of these respondents were significantly above those of the membership as a whole: private group median = $47,499, with a mean of $45,164, and private solo median = $52,499, with a mean of $49,739. Although this difference from the median for the entire membership may be significant, it is not clear whether the gross or net income was reported. If the gross income was reported, it was offset by the cost of office space and employee benefits (health insurance, retirement, life insurance, and professional liability coverage) that are often included as fringe benefits in other settings. Such deductions from gross income could reduce the net yearly income for private practitioners to an amount equal to or below the median of the overall membership who were working full-time.

Nevertheless, as Figure 6.6 shows, the proportion of members who reported higher income ranges in 1995 differed significantly according to the settings in which they practiced. A substantially higher percentage of the respondents in private solo and private group settings reported incomes above $70,000 (28.5 percent and 17.7 percent, respectively). The next highest proportions of respondents in this income range were in business–industry settings (9.4 percent), "other" (6.8 percent), and colleges–universities (6.5 percent). It is interesting that the respondents in these same settings also reported the highest percentage of incomes below $15,000.

Primary Income, by Primary Auspice of Employment

In 1995, the salaries of respondents in the public sector were, in general, higher than those of respondents in the private not-for-profit sector. These findings are consistent with those from 1991. Furthermore, respondents who worked for the federal government or military earned higher salaries than did those who worked for local or state governments. For example, 27.4 percent (323) of responding members who worked for the federal government and 21.4 percent (89) who worked for the military earned $45,000 to $49,999, but only

FIGURE 6.6

Percentage of NASW Members Reporting High and Low Income,
by Primary Setting, 1995

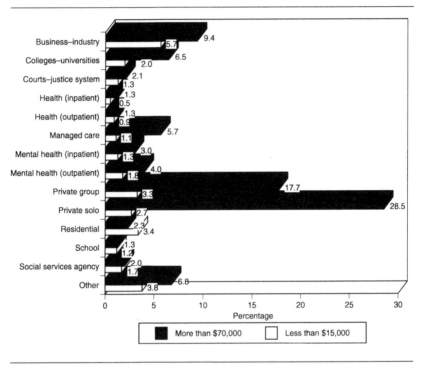

18.3 percent (1,408) employed by local governments and 17.1 percent
(983) employed by state governments earned that amount. However,
the highest incomes ($50,000 to $70,000 or more) were reported by
respondents in the private for-profit sector (see Table 6.9). The highest
mean reported income in 1995 was also for the private for-profit sector
($43,146).

The largest percentage of NASW members (58.2 percent, or 9,244)
employed by the private not-for-profit sector earned between $25,000
and $39,999. The largest proportion of NASW members earning
$45,000 or more were employed in the private for-profit sector, and
43.7 percent (549) of those earning $60,000 to $64,999 and 70.5
percent (1,538) of those earning $70,000 or more worked in the private
for-profit sector. A large majority of the respondents who listed their

143

TABLE 6.9

Primary Income of NASW Members, by Primary Auspice, 1995

Auspice	n	Percentage of Total	25th Percentile	Median	Mean	75th Percentile
			Annual Primary Income			
Private for-profit	9,398	23.3	$27,499	$37,499	$43,146	$52,499
Private not-for-profit	15,868	39.4	27,499	32,499	34,761	37,499
Public federal	1,178	2.9	32,499	37,499	39,636	47,499
Public local	7,697	19.1	27,499	32,499	36,474	47,499
Public military	415	1.0	32,499	37,499	39,451	47,499
Public state	5,739	14.2	27,499	32,499	36,471	47,499

Note: N = 40,295.

employment auspice as private for-profit were probably self-employed, given the growth in private independent practice.

Primary Income, by Primary Function

From 1986 to 1991, the mean income range by function remained stagnant, but the functions shifted rank in relation to each other. In 1995, the respondents with the primary functions of community organization–advocacy and clinical–direct service reported lower incomes than did those reporting other primary functions (see Table 6.10). Midway on the income continuum were those with primary functions in supervision, training, and policy. Respondents in administration, teaching, and research reported the highest mean incomes. These findings are consistent with earlier NASW studies. For example, Gibelman and Schervish (1993a) reported that the lowest incomes were for members in community organization–advocacy; salaries for those in administration–management, research, and teaching fell above the median; and the midrange incomes were for those in supervision.

The midrange salaries for respondents with direct service and community organizing primary functions were $32,499 to $42,499; for those in supervision, $32,499 to $47,499; and for those in training, $32,499 to $42,499. The midrange salaries of those in management were $32,499 to $52,499, with, as discussed later, a significant number earning salaries at the upper end of the continuum.

144

TABLE 6.10

Primary Income of NASW Members, by Primary Function, 1995

Function	n	Percentage of Total	Annual Primary Income			
			25th Percentile	Median	Mean	75th Percentile
Administration–management	7,447	17.9	$32,499	$47,499	$44,147	$52,499
Clinical–direct service	28,191	67.8	27,499	32,499	35,355	37,499
Community organizing–advocacy	66	0.2	27,499	32,499	34,620	42,499
Policy	312	0.8	27,499	37,499	38,445	47,499
Research	151	0.4	32,499	37,499	40,347	47,499
Supervision	2,800	6.7	32,499	37,499	37,269	47,499
Teaching	1,642	4.0	32,499	37,499	40,780	47,499
Training	26	0.1	32,499	37,499	38,076	42,499
Other	915	2.2	27,499	32,499	38,057	47,499

Note: $N = 41,550$.

These findings are again consistent with those of earlier NASW salary studies. Gibelman and Schervish (1993a) found that the highest mean salary ($48,265 in 1993) was earned by members with a primary function of university teaching, followed respectively by research (mean = $40,783) and management–administration (mean = $39,079). The lowest mean salary was found for those in community organization ($29,154), agency training ($31,556), and direct service ($31,729).

The primary functions of administration–management (7.4 percent), research (9.9 percent), and teaching (4.4 percent) had the highest proportion of respondents who reported incomes above $70,000 (see Figure 6.7). However, teaching, training and community organizing–advocacy had the largest percentages of members reporting the lowest levels of primary income. Of those reporting incomes of $60,000 to $64,999, 47.8 percent (617) were in clinical–direct service, and of those reporting incomes of above $70,000, 24.8 percent (550) were in clinical–direct service. Findings related to primary income by primary setting suggest that these high-income earners were in private solo or group practice.

FIGURE 6.7

Percentage of NASW Members Reporting High and Low Income, by
Primary Function, 1995

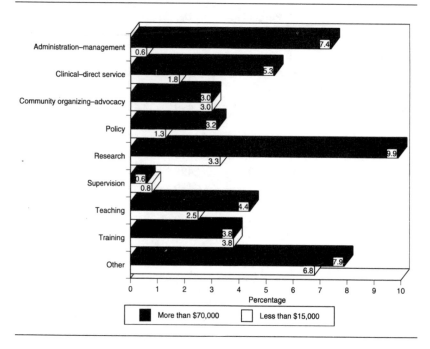

Also consistent is the finding that of those earning $70,000 or more, 28.3
percent (96) have a primary focus of individual–behavior.

The second largest proportion of members earning between $60,000
and $64,999 were in administration–management (38.7 percent, or
500), and of those reporting incomes of above $70,000, 24.8 percent
(550) were in administration–management.

Primary Income, by Region

There are discernible variations in income by region of the country in
which members practice. Members who reside in the New England,
Mid-Atlantic, South Atlantic, and Pacific states are more likely to earn
higher salaries. For example, in 1995, of those earning $60,000 to
$69,999, 28.2 percent (131) lived in the Mid-Atlantic states, 17.0
percent (79) lived in the South Atlantic states, and 16.3 (76) lived in the

Pacific states. Of those earning $70,000 or more, 30.0 percent (277) lived in the Mid-Atlantic states, 15.3 (141) lived in the South Atlantic states, and 17.7 (164) lived in the Pacific states. The proportion of respondents who earned incomes below the median of $25,000 to $29,999 in these three regions was also lower than the proportion of members earning low incomes in other regions. Incomes tended to be lower for those in the East South Central region, followed by the West South Central region (see Table 6.11).

SECONDARY INCOME

The income from secondary employment earned by NASW members employed full-time has remained consistently low since 1988, and the overwhelming majority of members did not report any secondary income in the three study years. (This finding may reflect the failure to complete the renewal questionnaire more than the absence of a secondary income.) Of the 12,605 respondents who reported a secondary income in 1995, 64.7 percent (8,156) earned less than $15,000 from that source, and only 9.9 percent (1,270) reported a secondary income of $20,000 or more. The proportions were similar for the 12,169 respondents in 1991: 66.8 percent (8,126) earned $4,999 or less, and 7.8 percent (950) earned $15,000 or more.

Income from secondary sources, however, has risen over time. In 1961, less than 10.0 percent of the NASW membership received remuneration from more than one job (Becker, 1961). This proportion rose to 29.6 percent (12,605 of the 42,610 data set) in 1995 compared with 29.5 percent in 1991 and 21.8 percent in 1988.

Secondary Income, by Gender

Similar to findings concerning primary income, gender disparities were also evident in relation to secondary income. For example, 68.5 percent (5,593) of women earned $15,000 or less from secondary sources compared with 57.1 percent (2,426) of men. However, in all secondary income categories above $15,000, men earned disproportionately more than women. For example, of the respondents earning between $25,000 and $29,999 in 1995, 4.3 percent (353) were women and 7.5 percent (320) were men.

Also noteworthy is the proportion of men who reported secondary earnings. Although the proportion of men working full-time consisted of only 25.1 percent of respondents (higher, however, than the proportion

147

TABLE 6.11

Primary Income of NASW Members, by Region, 1995

Region	n	Percentage of Total	Annual Primary Income			
			25th Percentile	Median	Mean	75th Percentile
East North Central	7,809	18.5	$27,499	$32,499	$35,657	$42,499
East South Central	1,539	3.6	22,499	32,499	32,709	37,499
Mid-Atlantic	9,743	23.1	27,499	37,499	39,529	47,499
Mountain	2,034	4.8	27,499	32,499	35,842	42,499
New England	4,069	9.6	27,499	32,499	37,928	47,499
Pacific	4,450	10.6	32,499	37,499	41,106	47,499
South Atlantic	6,396	15.2	27,499	32,499	36,738	47,499
Territories	1,369	3.2	27,499	32,499	35,961	47,499
West North Central	2,491	5.9	27,499	32,499	34,774	37,499
West South Central	2,268	5.4	27,499	32,499	35,385	37,499

Note: N = 42,168.

of men in the overall membership), more than 35 percent of those reporting secondary incomes were men.

Secondary Income, by Work Setting and Functions

Of those reporting a secondary income in 1995, 58.8 percent (5,147) worked in the private for-profit sector and 26.5 percent (2,323) worked in the not-for-profit sector as their secondary auspice. Fifty-one percent (5,382) of the 10,556 respondents to the questions about secondary income and secondary function reported that they engaged in clinical–direct service as their secondary function. These data suggest that the majority of NASW members who earn a secondary income do so in private solo or group practice. Indeed, of the 10,057 members who responded to the questions about secondary income and secondary setting, 53.1 percent (5,346) reported their secondary setting to be private group or private solo practice. These findings are also consistent with secondary income by secondary practice area: Those with a secondary income of over $25,000 are overwhelmingly represented among those with a secondary practice of mental health.

CHAPTER HIGHLIGHTS

- The midrange of the primary income reported by NASW members working full-time was $27,499 to $42,499 and the median income was $34,215, up from $31,264 in 1991.
- Compared with the income reported in the 1961 salary study, income reported by members in 1995 has not kept pace with inflation.
- The increase in salaries from 1987 to 1995 was less than the rate of inflation.
- In 1995, the salaries reported by NASW members were significantly lower than those reported by others employed in professional and technical positions in the country, and the primary incomes of members are growing at a slower rate than those of their professional and technical counterparts.
- The primary income of the members is affected by their highest social work degree, year of degree, experience, and age. However, experience, year of degree, and age are related to each other.
- Reported incomes rise fastest during the first five years of practice. Also, NASW members appear to reach an income plateau after about 10 years of practice, after which increases in income are negligible.
- A disproportionate number of members with a primary practice of aging, children–family, and occupational social work earn salaries below the median, while a disproportionate number of members in mental health, occupational social work, and other earn salaries above the median.
- There is evidence of a significant gender bias in the incomes reported by the members: Men earn more and are disproportionately overrepresented at the higher end of the income range, and women are disproportionately overrepresented at the lower end.
- Those working in settings related to business and in residential settings (such as group homes and nursing homes) reported incomes at the low end of the income range in all three study years, whereas those working in settings related to private solo and private group practice and in universities reported incomes at the high end.
- Members with a primary function in administration, research, and teaching tended to earn higher salaries than those in other functional areas.

- Those working in private practice reported the highest mean and ceiling incomes, but their incomes may not include adjustments for overhead and employee benefits.
- Except for workers in private practice, government workers reported higher incomes than did nongovernment workers.
- Members who worked in the New England, Mid-Atlantic, and Pacific regions reported higher incomes, and those who worked in the U.S. territories and in the East South Central and West North Central regions reported lower incomes than did those in other regions of the country.
- The majority of members who reported income from secondary sources cited the private for-profit sector as their secondary auspice of practice.
- Private (group or solo) practice is the predominant source of secondary income.
- Of those reporting secondary income, the vast majority earned less than $15,000 per year.
- Compared with the membership as a whole, a disproportionate number of men reported a secondary income.

REFERENCES

Becker, R. (1961). *Study of salaries of NASW members*. New York: National Association of Social Workers.

Belon, C. J., & Gould, K. H. (1977). Not even equals: Sex-related inequities. *Social Work, 22,* 466–471.

Bureau of Labor Statistics. (1996a). Consumer Price Indexes, All Items Series, Internet address http://www.stats.bls.gov

Bureau of Labor Statistics. (1996b). *Current population survey: Usual weekly earnings of wage and salary workers, first quarter 1996*. Washington, DC: Author.

Declining wages for high school and college graduates. (1992, July 12). *Washington Post*, p. H2.

Fanshel, D. (1976). Status differentials: Men and women in social work. *Social Work, 21,* 448–455.

Fortune, A. E., & Hanks, L. L. (1988). Gender inequities in early social work careers. *Social Work, 33,* 221–226.

Gibelman, M., & Schervish, P. (1993a). *What we earn: 1993 NASW salary survey*. Washington, DC: National Association of Social Workers.

Gibelman, M., & Schervish, P. (1993b). *Who we are: A profile of the social work labor force as reflected in the NASW membership*. Washington, DC: National Association of Social Workers.

Gibelman, M., & Schervish, P. (1995). Pay equity in social work: Not! *Social Work, 40,* 622–629.

Gould, K. H., & Bok-Lim, C. K. (1976). Salary inequities between men and women in schools of social work: Myth or reality? *Journal of Education for Social Work, 12,* 50–55.

Jennings, P. L., & Daley, M. (1979). Sex discrimination in social work careers. *Social Work Research & Abstracts, 15,* 17–21.

Landers, S. (1992, April). Survey eyes therapy fees. *NASW News,* pp. 1, 8.

Membership survey shows practice shifts (1983, November). *NASW News,* pp. 6–7.

National Association of Social Workers. (1987). *Salaries in social work: A summary report on the salaries of NASW members, July 1986–June 1987.* Silver Spring, MD: Author.

Scotch, C. B. (1971). Sex status in social work: Grist for women's liberation. *Social Work, 16,* 5–11.

Sowers-Hoag, K. M., & Harrison, D. F. (1991). Women in social work education: Progress or promise? *Journal of Social Work Education, 27,* 320–328.

Strobino, J., & McCoy, M. (1992). Recruitment, retention and promotion: Management issues related to salary equity. In L. M. Healy & B. A. Pine (Eds.), *Managers' choices* (pp. 27–43). Boca Raton, FL: National Network for Social Work Managers.

Sutton, J. A. (1982). Sex discrimination among social workers. *Social Work, 27,* 211–217.

Yamatani, H. (1982). Gender and salary inequity: Statistical interaction effects. *Social Work Research & Abstracts, 18,* 24–27.

York, R. O. (1987). Sexual discrimination in social work: Is it salary or advancement? *Social Work, 32,* 336–339.

CHAPTER 7

WHERE WE ARE GOING

TRENDS AND ISSUES

The findings presented in this book allow for the identification of a number of trends and issues regarding the composition of the profession, the scope of the members' professional roles, and changes in the nature of practice. This chapter discusses some of these trends and issues and their implications for the profession and for NASW.

FEMINIZATION OF THE PROFESSION

The trend toward an increasing proportion of women in the NASW membership has been consistent and is growing, as illustrated in Figure 7.1. The trend is mirrored among the larger population of social workers. The proportion of all social work positions held by women was 57.0 percent in 1960, 64.0 percent in 1983, 65.0 percent in 1987, 68.0 percent in 1991, and 69.3 percent in 1994 (BLS, 1961, 1991, 1994).

There is a clear indication that the proportion of women in social work will continue to increase. Of the 24,536 juniors and seniors enrolled full-time in baccalaureate social work programs in Fall 1994, 85.3 percent were women. For full- and part-time master's degree students enrolled as of fall 1994, 81.9 percent were female (Lennon, 1995). The next cohort of professionals entering social work practice will thus reflect an increasing female dominance.

The dominance of women in the social work profession and NASW is not the issue, per se. Rather, the issue is the impact of this female dominance on the status of the profession in light of this society's devaluation of women, their role in society, and their professional contributions. Historically, the effects of these societal biases have been

FIGURE 7.1

Proportion of Female to Male NASW Members, 1961–1995

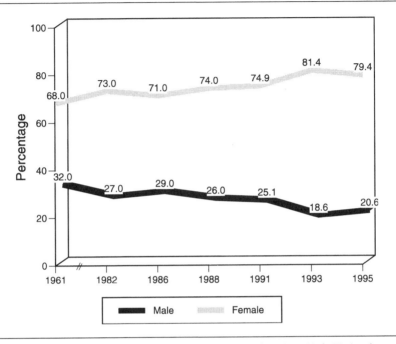

Sources: Becker, R. (1961). *Study of salaries of NASW members*. New York: National Association of Social Workers; Gibelman, M., & Schervish, P. (1993). The glass ceiling in social work: Is it shatterproof? *Affilia, 8,* 442–455; Gibelman, M., & Schervish, P. (1993). *Who we are: The social work labor force as reflected in the NASW membership.* Washington, DC: NASW Press; National Association of Social Workers. (1987). *Salaries in social work: A summary report on the salaries of NASW members, July 1986–June 1987.* Silver Spring, MD: Author.

observed in female-dominated professions, including teaching and nursing (Etzioni, 1969). Women, and the professions they dominate, have received lower salaries and have been held in less social esteem than have men and the professions they dominate.

Salary disparities by gender and profession, described later, continue to be an issue for the social work profession and for NASW and its members. Similarly, the tendency for male NASW members to hold proportionately more management positions raises serious questions of equity and parity in the profession.

153

YOUTH AND INEXPERIENCE OF THE MEMBERSHIP

The median age range of NASW members for all three study years (1988, 1991, and 1995) was 41 to 45. The proportion of members age 51 and over decreased from 1988 to 1995, whereas the proportion of members under age 30 increased significantly.

Trends in social work education offer one explanation for the large and growing proportion of younger NASW members. These trends include the growth in the number of baccalaureate and graduate social work education programs, a dramatic increase in the number of part-time degree students, and the increased demand for off-campus and extension programs (Beless, 1995; Bernard, 1987). These trends, it can be assumed, would not occur if there was not an actual or potential student market.

CSWE (Lennon, 1995) reported that enrollments in accredited social work degree–granting programs are on the increase. With the exception of 1989, full-time enrollments in master's programs have increased each year since 1986. Enrollment of part-time MSW students has shown a similar rise, and doctoral enrollment also continues to rise steadily.

NASW has taken many steps to recruit new members from among the student population. Promotional information is routinely distributed to all graduate and undergraduate social work education programs to encourage students to join the association. In addition, the membership fee for students is discounted because NASW considers the recruitment of students to be an investment in the future. The rationale is clear, but the results are less certain.

In 1988, 12.8 percent of the total NASW membership consisted of individuals reporting student status. Despite intensive recruitment efforts, this proportion remained unchanged in 1991, although the absolute number of student members did rise. By 1995, the results of recruitment efforts were slightly more evident. In that year, 15.0 percent (23,156) of the total membership was composed of BSW, MSW, or PhD–DSW students.

Age usually reflects experience, but not among the NASW members. Perhaps because of career shifts or the patterns of education that are consistent with a female-dominated profession, NASW members tend to complete their highest degrees later in life than do people in other professions. Consequently, the members' level of experience is not necessarily what their ages would suggest. However, the relationship between age and experience is growing more apparent. From 1988 to 1995, the proportion of members with fewer than two years of experience rose dramatically, whereas the proportion of members with more than 15 years of experience fell considerably. Traditionally, one effect of downturns in the economy is that students stay in school longer and go on to graduate school sooner after they complete their undergraduate degrees. Thus, the shifts in the age and experience of NASW members between 1988 and 1995 may have been a result of anomalies in higher education because of recent economic downturns. This pattern may begin to reverse after 1995, as a result of actual and potential cutbacks in federal and state support for human services.

Another explanation for the growing proportion of young NASW members has to do with the retention of members. The proportion of younger members may be just as much a reflection of the decrease in older members through attrition than to trends in the educational system. If this speculation is true, the question is whether this attrition is a result of (1) the natural aging of the membership or (2) the abandonment of the profession by older members, who may seek more lucrative employment in other professions. A third possibility is that some members cease to consider NASW membership relevant to their needs and interests as they progress in their careers. Whatever the basis of the phenomenon, it is of utmost importance to NASW and the professionals it represents. Clearly, studies on lapsed members are necessary.

MULTICULTURAL CHARACTERISTICS

NASW is standing still in its efforts to attract ethnically diverse populations to the profession. In 1995, 87.9 percent of the full NASW membership was white, compared with 88.1 percent in 1991 and 88.4 percent in 1988. Thus, between 1988 and 1995 the proportion of people of color among the membership has remained relatively stable. African Americans constituted the second largest ethnic group in the membership, at 5.7 percent in 1995.

The larger social work labor force is faring better in the proportion of people of color. In 1995, 27.6 percent of all those holding social work–titled positions were people of color, of which 24.1 percent were African American (BLS, 1994). In 1991, 29.1 percent of all those holding social work–titled positions were African American or Hispanic (the only two ethnic groups for which statistics were reported) compared with 23.3 percent in 1984. Thus, the proportion of people of color within the larger social work labor force shows some fluctuation, but no substantial gain. It is not known what proportion of the ethnic groups represented in the BLS data are professionally trained social workers. The numbers do suggest, however, that NASW lags behind in its recruitment of people of color compared with the social services labor force as a whole.

Within social work education, the picture is somewhat more positive. Between 1969 and 1987, there was a steady decline in the proportion of people of color among MSW students, from 21.6 percent of full-time students to 13.9 percent (Spaulding, 1991). However, the trend seems to be reversing. Students from ethnic populations received 19.2 percent of the MSW degrees awarded in 1994. In 1994, 21.5 percent of full-time MSW students and 23.1 percent of part-time MSW students were people of color (Lennon, 1995). These statistics suggest that the current composition of students in social work education programs more closely mirrors the higher proportions of people of color evidenced in 1969 than in the 1970s and 1980s.

The two primary issues for the profession in this regard are the underrepresentation of people of color in social work and the lower proportion of NASW members of color compared with their numbers in the social services labor force.

The recruitment of people of color into the profession has become more challenging than in earlier years, primarily because of the increased openness and accessibility of other professions to members of ethnic groups. With these increased opportunities, it may be surmised that people of color are choosing careers in other, often more lucrative, fields. A compounding factor is social work's decreased emphasis on advocacy. Williams (1987) supported this view:

> Trends since the mid-1970s suggest that the profession will do even less for these minority groups as resources grow more scarce and as schools of social work gear up to respond to the needs of a current wave of recruits who are interested in family counseling and individual psychotherapy. These recruits indicate a distaste for advocacy and for the case management and resource provision skills that are traditional in working with disadvantaged groups and minorities. (p. 344)

Given the number of professional organizations and special-interest groups that have a direct bearing on the practice of social work, it is likely that many NASW members belong to more than one association. Tourse (1995) noted that there are several types of special-interest associations that may attract social workers, including those concerned with common service populations or types of agencies (for example, the Child Welfare League of America), those with specialized interests within the field (for example, National Association of Oncology Social Workers), and those whose focus of concern is on particular racial or ethnic groups (for example, the National Association of Black Social Workers [NABSW]).

It is likely that a proportion of NASW members belong to specialized function associations or to other organizations that, in most instances, complement and further the services and objectives of NASW. Other social workers, however, may choose to belong to one of the other types of special-interest associations rather than joining or maintaining membership in NASW. Tourse (1995) noted that

> there are divergent views within and among groups in social work, and interests sometimes do conflict or are discordant. These conflicts can be positive, however, in that they can stimulate further organizational and professional growth. (p. 2316)

It is not known whether people of color do not join NASW because they join other associations, if they join both NASW and other associations, or if they simply do not join any association.

The membership of NABSW was over 10,000 in 1987 (Williams, 1987). But in 1996, NABSW reported only 3,000 members (personal communication with H. Barbson, executive director, NABSW, July 1996), significantly lower than the 6,443 African American members of NASW in 1995. The drop in NABSW membership is not readily explainable.

The populations with which social workers work are often composed of disenfranchised people, including immigrants, members of ethnic and racial groups, women, and poor people. As a predominantly white profession (87.9 percent of the NASW membership in 1995), social work needs to develop and perfect the theories and tools that multicultural practice requires. More effective recruitment strategies are also essential to attract people of color into the profession.

WITHDRAWAL FROM PUBLIC SERVICE ROLE

In 1961, government at the federal, state, or municipal level was the major employer of NASW members. Becker (1961) found that "contrary to the long-held belief that the most highly trained social workers tend not to favor employment in the public services, the survey of NASW members shows that more than 52 percent work for federal, state, county, and municipal governmental agencies" (p. 5).

From 1961 to 1995, this situation changed significantly. Declassification (the reduction in standards of professional education and work-related experience for public social services jobs) has been a formidable challenge to the profession (Pecora & Austin, 1983). In 1993, the NASW Delegate Assembly adopted a policy statement on declassification (NASW, 1994) that noted:

> Public social service departments have failed to recognize the profession of social work as a major contributor to effective social services and as an advocate for social welfare policies and programs in the United States. Systematically, social workers are being eliminated from direct services, supervision, policy making, and administrative positions. This elimination is being accomplished by declassifying and reclassifying traditional social work positions in public-sector agencies. (p. 76)

Data on the primary practice settings of employed NASW members in the public sector reinforce the view that clients with the most complex and intractable socioeconomic and psychosocial problems are being provided service by the least educated of the NASW members. An increasing proportion of social workers working within public social services are at the BSW level, perhaps because of limited opportunities for them in the for-profit or not-for-profit sectors or because some undergraduate programs emphasize preparation for public sector employment (Gibelman & Schervish, 1996).

In general, the pay social workers receive in the public sector is higher than in the not-for-profit sector. Conditions of work and status issues within the workforce thus seem to be the determinant factors. Specht and Courtney (1994) noted that the conditions for social workers in public social services agencies are unpleasant and even dangerous at times. The physical setting of many public social services offices is often unattractive and uncomfortable and typically is located in the least-desirable sections of cities. The cumbersome rules and regulations and civil service procedures that govern the work of the public-sector social worker are frustrating to many social workers and reduce the time and attention for direct services delivery (Gibelman & Schervish, 1996). The social control functions that must be carried out to protect children and certain dependent adults are also at odds with the enabling and helping role with which social workers identify (Specht & Courtney, 1994).

Cutbacks in federal funds for training, which supported many public welfare employees through MSW programs during the 1960s, also had an impact on the number of graduates entering or returning to public social services employment (Gibelman, 1983). Meanwhile, other social work specialties, primarily private practice, were gaining ground. The growth in private practice was also attributable to external forces, such as third-party vendorship, made possible by more states offering licensure to social workers. Thus, the role of NASW members in public social services was affected by the de-emphasis on social work intervention in the public sector and the concurrent increase of professional opportunities in other sectors. These shifts had the longer term effect of altering the demographics of the clientele with whom NASW members and other social workers traditionally worked: poor and disenfranchised people.

The trend to declassify may also be affecting the human services job market in general (Gibelman, 1995). Many current classified advertisements under the category of "social work" list the bachelor's degree as the baseline requirement, with a master's degree cited as "desirable" or "preferred." This trend may relate to administrative issues. For example, by not listing a degree as a requirement, employers have greater flexibility in their hiring decisions. Also, the hiring of less experienced or less educated personnel may be a way to control agency costs (Gibelman, 1995). The current fiscal constraints felt by most human services agencies may lead them to hire social workers who cost less— those holding a BSW as opposed to an MSW, the less experienced versus the more experienced practitioner (Gibelman, 1995).

Ironically, despite the dramatic downward trend in the proportion of social workers employed by government at any level over the past 30 years, the involvement of social workers in government is on the increase. The majority of social services in this country are provided by voluntary agencies under purchase-of-service arrangements; government remains the chief financier of services (Gibelman, 1995). In addition, many private practitioners depend on third-party payments, such as Medicaid, for their income (Ginsberg, 1988).

PREDOMINANCE OF MENTAL HEALTH PRACTICE

The largest proportion of NASW members identify a primary practice area of mental health. In 1995, 38.3 percent of employed respondents indicated that mental health was their primary practice area, up from 35.5 percent in 1991 and 34.5 percent in 1988 (Gibelman & Schervish, 1993b).

Some estimates show that social workers are the dominant providers of mental health services in this country. In about 1,000 counties, that is, in one-third of the counties in the country, social workers are the only licensed providers of mental health services (Goldstein, 1994). As much as 65 percent of all psychotherapy and mental health services are provided by social workers (Goldstein, 1993). Conversely, 47 percent of responding social workers indicated the primary focus of their practice as individual–behavioral problems or family issues. As a focus of practice, less than 2.5 percent of respondents indicated a focus on social resource factors such as income, housing, and employment.

The overriding predominance of mental health as a specialization within social work is not likely to abate. Data on the primary fields of practice and social problem concentrations selected by master's students enrolled in social work education programs for the 1993–1994 academic year are shown in Table 7.1.

Although there is a large proportion of students in the "not yet determined" or "none, methods concentration only" categories, data on the declared areas of practice of MSW students are remarkably consistent with the statistical profile of the 1995 NASW membership. Family services and child welfare, when combined, ranks first among primary fields of practice, followed closely by mental health and, lagging behind but still a major area, health. The dearth of social workers concentrating in aging, alcohol–drugs, community organization, occupational social work, and managed care shows a consistent pattern with the proportion of social workers represented in these areas among the NASW membership.

The predominance of social workers in mental health, however, is accompanied by other trends noted in this chapter. These include the decrease in the proportion of social workers in public agency practice and in such fields as corrections, juvenile justice, and public welfare. These changes are ripe for professional debate. They are, in themselves, neither good nor bad, but the profession may wish to consider the short- and long-term implications of social work becoming increasingly associated and perhaps synonymous with mental health practice. The issue is all the more salient given the increase in the proportion of NASW members in private practice.

INCREASE IN PRIVATE PRACTICE

Social work has traditionally been practiced in organizational settings. The history of the profession has been marked by a consistent and dual

Where We Are Going

TABLE 7.1

Concentrations Selected by Enrolled Social Work Students,
Academic Year 1993–1994

Concentration	Number Enrolled
Aging–gerontological social work	646
Alcohol, drug, or substance abuse	522
Child welfare	2,131
Community planning	186
Corrections–criminal justice	230
Family services	2,599
Group services	128
Health	2,239
Mental health or community mental health	3,514
Mental retardation	131
Occupational–industrial social work	225
Public assistance–public welfare	88
Rehabilitation	60
School social work	883
Other	1,353
Combinations	313
Not yet determined	6,873
None (methods concentration only)	8,024
Total	30,145

Source: Lennon, T. M. (1995). *Statistics on social work education in the United States: 1994.* Alexandria, VA: Council on Social Work Education. Used with permission of CSWE.

tension between a focus on the individual and a focus on the environment. This dynamic tension can be construed, in terms of practice, as a blend of functions that focus on individuals and on advocacy (Hopps & Pinderhughes, 1987). One way to resolve the tension between the constraints of institutional structures and the commitment to serving human needs may be evident in the trend toward independent practice. The data reveal that private practice has become an increasingly important alternative for the provision of social work services.

The private practice of social work has been defined as "the process in which the values, knowledge, and skills of social work, acquired through sufficient education and experience, are used to deliver social work services autonomously to clients in exchange for mutually agreed

161

payment" (Barker, 1995b, p. 294). In private or proprietary practice, the social worker is employed directly by the client and is paid by the client either directly or through a vendorship arrangement. Private practitioners usually provide for their own offices, personnel benefits, staff support, record keeping, and so on.

Private practice is predominantly focused on the direct delivery of clinical social services. The circumstances under which private practice is carried out are influenced by the policies of the states regulating it, the standards of professional associations, and the insurance companies that determine reimbursement rates (Karger & Stoesz, 1994).

The proportion of members engaged in private practice increased from 10.9 percent in 1982 to 15.3 percent in 1987 (NASW, 1987). Unfortunately, these data do not differentiate between primary and secondary practice or between solo and group private practice. By 1988, the proportion of employed NASW members in private solo and group primary practice was 14.8 percent and in secondary practice 45.8 percent. In 1991, 16.8 percent of NASW members cited private solo and group as their primary areas of practice and 45.8 percent cited these as their secondary areas. By 1995, the proportion of members citing private solo and group as their primary areas of practice had risen to 19.7 percent, with 45.5 percent identifying them as their secondary areas.

Disillusionment with agency-based practice, economic need, desire to gain control over working conditions, and interest in concentrating on clinical work with particular populations or types of presenting problems have been cited as some of the motivating reasons for the growth in private practice (Abramovitz, 1986; Jayaratne, Davis-Sacks, & Chess, 1991; Saxton, 1988). Many social workers pursue a career in private practice to escape the bureaucratic constraints of many public service jobs. Some want a higher income with more freedom to determine their own schedules and clientele (Barker, 1995a). Furthermore, cutbacks in funding for social services agencies have greatly reduced the number of available positions, thereby forcing some social workers into private practice simply to remain in their chosen profession (Barker, 1995a).

Although the data show that private practitioners do quite well financially compared with social workers in other settings, there are also negatives to consider. First, the expense of establishing and maintaining a private practice can be large, and the income is often unpredictable. Typically, less than half of the money social workers collect from clients is spendable; most goes for overhead expenses such as taxes, health and other insurance, education, and retirement (Barker, 1995a).

The private practice of social work is controversial within the profession. The arguments against private practice have focused on value conflicts with professional ethos, including discrimination against less affluent people and failure to provide services to those who cannot pay (Barker, 1992; Karger, 1989; Merle, 1962). Other arguments include the potential depletion of social workers in agencies where they are needed and the importance of agency norms and standards for the practice of social work (Barker, 1992).

The issue of fee-for-service in the private sector has been the subject of substantial debate among social workers. Specht and Courtney (1994) unequivocally viewed this movement within the profession as negative: "We believe that social work has abandoned its mission to help the poor and oppressed and to build communality" (p. 4). In their view, community problems are increasing while social work as a profession is devoting itself more and more to "the psychotherapeutic enterprise." The profession now seeks overridingly to "perfect the individual" rather than acting on the belief in the "perfectibility of society."

To counter these arguments, private practitioners argue that clearly defined roles and activities can exist in private practice and that, in fact, the need to provide potential consumers with information about their services makes role clarification and delineation essential (Barker, 1992). They also argue that agencies select the clients they wish to serve on the basis of ability to pay or some type of means test, or on the basis of religion, ethnicity, type of disability, or other personal characteristic, such as gender (Barker, 1992). Concerns about depleting the agency-based labor force have not been borne out (Williams & Hopps, 1990).

Despite criticism from within and outside the profession, private practice continues to be a popular form of practice. Although the merits and pitfalls of the private practice of social work have been debated for years, the debate should now logically focus on the following implications of private practice:

- What are the consequences of private practice on the profession and for the delivery of services: who gets served, with what types of interventions, for how long, and with what outcomes?
- What are the career paths, salaries, and demographics of private practitioners compared with other social workers?
- As private practice takes on a distinctly individual-oriented nature, how does the profession reconcile its role in and commitment to the development of social policy and the management of the service delivery system?

- How do private practitioners honor a professional code of ethics that not only requires services to individuals but delineates social workers' responsibility to make larger social systems more responsive to the needs of individuals?

Of particular importance to the future of private practice is the health care reform movement. Although health care reform legislation has thus far been rejected by Congress, new proposals are likely to surface. A key question is whether and to what extent social workers will be included as care providers in the legislation that finally is passed. What is clear is that health care reform will impose limitations on the nature and extent of health and mental health practice (Gibelman & Schervish, in press). For example, among the considerations in the array of health care proposals considered in 1994 was a limit on outpatient psychotherapy and higher copayments for psychotherapy. Limitations on inpatient and residential treatment coverage were also considered (Hiratsuka, 1994).

A potential trend that should be closely monitored is whether and to what extent social work's role within the managed care industry will grow. In 1994, NASW added managed care to its data collection form as one of the primary settings of practice. For 1995, however, only 0.3 percent (226) of the employed NASW membership cited managed care as their primary setting. Within this vastly expanding and significant industry, the question becomes: What is social work's role?

GROWTH IN THE PRIVATE FOR-PROFIT SECTOR

The third sector of social welfare—for-profit enterprises—is expanding, as is social workers' role within it. Although for-profit social welfare activities, as carried out in private for-profit hospitals, nursing homes, and child care facilities, have existed for a long time, the growth in for-profit social welfare in recent years has been explosive (Macarov, 1991). This growth is reflected in the NASW membership: In 1995, 27.1 percent of employed NASW members worked in the private for-profit sector, up from 22.2 percent in 1991 and 18.5 percent in 1988. The trend is consistent and strong.

Proprietary social services are social services delivered for profit. The most frequent form of for-profit practice in social work is independent or private clinical practice. But proprietary practice also includes some areas of macro practice, such as consultation, organizing of special-interest groups, and agencies targeted to meet the needs of special populations, such as home care combined with social services for elderly people (Barker, 1992).

Privatization has become extremely popular among elected leaders and citizens as a way to divest government of some of its functions. Support for this movement continues to be strong. The privatization of human services has led to the creation of a new and growing network of proprietary agencies ready to provide competitive services, often under contract with government agencies or benefiting from third-party reimbursement, through Medicare, Medicaid, or private insurance.

The opportunities for social workers to practice in for-profit settings are growing. Because for-profits have as their "bottom line" the goal of making a profit, services may be modified to achieve this goal. To what extent clients may receive different, less effective, or perhaps better quality services is as yet unclear. The debate on privatization, in fact, includes consideration of the ultimate impact on the quality and quantity of services (see Abramovitz, 1986; Karger & Stoesz, 1994; Macarov, 1991).

MACRO-LEVEL SOCIAL WORK PRACTICE

The proportion of NASW members whose positions involve the primary or secondary functions of policy, research, or community organization is negligible. Although management is better represented as a primary function among the members than are the other macro areas of practice, only 15.5 percent of the 1995 employed members' primary function is in management. These findings contradict the traditional wisdom about the extent of vertical and horizontal mobility in the profession.

One explanation for these data may be simply that social workers in macro practice do not join NASW or that they let their membership lapse because they think that membership in NASW is not relevant to their work or that another association represents their interests better. Another explanation may be that only a small proportion of social workers perform policy, research, or community organization functions and hold such positions. Supporting this latter view is the increasing trend of public and not-for-profit social services agencies to hire people trained in business and public administration for management. A third explanation may be that, either by choice or because of shifts in the job market, the movement to private practice is focused more on interventions at the individual level than at the macro level.

Several commentators observe and lament the decreased role of social work in social policy, planning, and advocacy (see Specht &

Courtney, 1994), and others urge a more active role for social workers in the political realm (Ewalt, 1994). The direction of the NASW membership, however, as reflected in data from 1988 to 1995, is clearly away from macro practice.

PART-TIME EMPLOYMENT

Another emerging trend in the social work labor market, as evident in the gradual but consistent change in NASW membership, is the increase in the proportion of part-time employees. From the vantage point of employing agencies, the motives are clear: In an era of cutback, employers seek to keep personnel costs down. Hiring two part-time employees can be substantially less expensive than hiring one full-time worker because part-time employees are not entitled to the same level of fringe benefits as are full-time employees (Gibelman, 1995).

Another variation in the labor market that promotes part-time employment is the use of per diem or per-contracted-job employment. For example, a social worker may be hired by an adoption agency to do home studies and be paid on the basis of each completed home study. Or a social worker may be retained to provide in-home services on a case-by-case basis. As social services agencies are forced to seek cost savings, the use of part-time employees is likely to increase (Gibelman, 1995).

DEVIATION FROM NASW'S RECOMMENDED SALARIES

The salaries reported by NASW members who were employed full-time in 1995 fell short of the levels recommended by NASW in 1990 when adjusted for inflation, a deviation also evident in 1988 and 1991. However, the 1995 median income has come into closer alignment with the recommended salaries.

This deviation has historical roots. The 1961 NASW salary study (Becker, 1961) reported that "the worker with ten to fifteen years of experience is earning a median salary of $7,500; considerably less than the goal of $10,000 set by NASW salary standards for experienced and competent workers with ten years of experience" (p. 4).

Salaries have remained stagnant. When adjusted for inflation, the 1961 and 1988 median salaries of NASW members were virtually identical (Gibelman & Schervish, 1993b). The "stand still" nature of social work salaries continues. The 1995 salaries have actually lost ground compared with the 1988 median reported income of full-time, working members.

In the years immediately following the creation of NASW in 1955, the association focused on attracting and maintaining members "through an appeal to their need for status and improved salaries" (Beck, 1977, p. 1090). In 1957, NASW began its periodic publication of minimum salary standards (Battle, 1987). Social workers' low pay has been a long-standing concern and has been the object of strategic planning by NASW since the association's inception. It remains a major item on NASW's agenda.

Beyond the generally lower-than-average professional salaries of NASW members is the internal issue of gender-based bias in members' incomes. In 1961, 32.0 percent of the members were male and earned a median salary of $7,700 compared with female members' median salary of $6,600 (Becker, 1961). The 1986–1987 salary study (NASW, 1987) revealed that, on average, male respondents earned about 30.5 percent more than female respondents. These disparities held true for the 1988 and 1991 membership. By 1995, with substantial societal attention focused on the glass ceiling and pay equity issues (Gibelman & Schervish, 1993a, 1995), the situation within the NASW membership still shows no improvement.

An analysis of variance of primary income by gender for 1995, controlling for experience, degree, function, practice, ethnicity, geographic location, and licensing, indicated that gender was a significant factor in the variances. As much as 12 percent ($4,350) of the differential in primary income could be accounted for by gender (see Table 7.2).

In a stepwise multiple regression, gender accounted for more of the differential in primary income than did auspice, setting, practice, function, licensing, or region (see Table 7.3). The only two factors exerting a greater influence than gender on income were experience and degree. Ethnicity and area of practice were found to have no significant impact.

CHANGING VOCABULARY

Casework has traditionally been the predominant method of social work practice. But in 1980, Minahan (1980) asked, "What is clinical social work?" She noted that the term "clinical social work" had emerged in the profession's vocabulary in the 1970s as a euphemism for social casework, treatment-oriented social group work, social treatment, psychiatric social work, and direct practice.

There are several implications of this changing vocabulary for the study of NASW members' characteristics and for any research on the nature of social work practice. To achieve an accurate description of

167

TABLE 7.2

Analysis of Variance of Income of NASW Members, by Gender, 1995

Source of Variation	Sum of Squares	df	F	Significance
Covariates				
Auspice	429.9	1	96.0	<.01
Combined	5358.5	7	170.9	<.01
Ethnic	47.3	1	10.5	<.01
Function	3,122.6	1	697.3	<.01
Licensing	339.2	1	75.7	<.01
Practice	87.1	1	19.5	<.01
Region	593.6	1	132.6	<.01
Setting	578.6	1	129.2	<.01
Main Effects				
Explained	6,096.9	8	170.2	<.10
Gender	738.4	1	164.9	<.01
Residual	23,241.3	5,190		
Total	29,338.1	5,198		

Multiple Comparison			

Grand Mean = 6.41

Variable	n	Unadjusted Deviation Eta	Adjusted Deviation Beta
Gender			
Female	3,886	−.27	−.22
Male	1,313	.81	.65
		.20	.16
Multiple R squared			.20
Multiple R			.45

TABLE 7.3

Multiple Regression of Factors Affecting Income of NASW Members, 1995

Factor	B	SE B	Beta	T	Significance of T
Auspice	.16	.01	.13	10.7	<.01
Degree	.65	.09	.08	6.9	<.01
Experience	.53	.02	.38	32.7	<.01
Function	.17	.01	.20	18.1	<.01
Gender	–.47	.06	–.08	–7.9	<.01
Licensing	.29	.08	.04	3.6	<.01
Region	.14	.01	.16	15.6	<.01
Setting	.10	.01	.18	13.6	<.01
Constant	.15	.21		.7	.45

Note: Ethnicity and Practice were not included in the equation.

where social workers work, what they do, and at what level of practice, NASW members must describe the same phenomena from the same perspective and with a common vocabulary. The popularity of Barker's (1995b) *Social Work Dictionary* suggests that students and practitioners alike recognize the need for a common vocabulary.

The new demographic data form inaugurated by NASW in 1994 seeks to update and simplify the vocabulary. For example, the new data collection form asks about "type of organization" rather than "auspice." However, there may still be a lack of common understanding of such terms as "practice setting" and "function." The repeated use of these terms in the social work literature to describe the same phenomena must be encouraged. For example, if "clinical practice" is the preferred term, then authors and editors must be required to use it, and "casework" and "psychiatric social work" must be dropped from the vocabulary and used only as historical terms.

Chapters 4 and 5 addressed the potential for confusion about the differentiation between primary and secondary settings of practice and auspice and primary and secondary functions. But the lack of a standard vocabulary may be far more pervasive. For example, what exactly is management? The face validity of this and other terms used in social work surveys should be determined. Are NASW members describing the same phenomenon? Similarly, it should not be assumed that the meanings of "for-profit services" and "nonprofit organizations" are commonly understood.

Definitional issues affect the validity and reliability of any reports about the composition and nature of the work of the social work labor force. Steps must be taken to ensure that the vocabulary of the profession is standardized and understood by its members.

FUTURE DIRECTIONS

The trends that emerged from this study of the characteristics of NASW members suggest that the profession and NASW need to consider how to

- recruit people of color and men
- identify clients served by social workers in different settings of practice and the implications for achieving the mission and goals of the profession
- use social workers at the three educational levels—BSW, MSW, and PhD–DSW—to deal with the more intractable social problems and at-risk clients
- reassert a more active public sector role
- influence social work students and practitioners to practice at the macro level
- achieve equity and parity in the salaries of men and women
- help women in social work overcome the "glass ceiling"
- improve the preparation of practitioners for vertical and horizontal mobility in the profession, for example, in response to changes in functions and in practice settings
- reconcile the needs of practitioners for independence and self-actualization with the profession's role and mission to serve the most disadvantaged members of society
- ascertain the actual and potential impact of managed care on social work practice and determine a role for social work within the managed care industry.

With the exceptions of managed care and the glass ceiling, we listed these same agenda items in 1993. Their consistency and tenacity suggest an even more urgent mandate for the profession and the association that represents it.

Where We Are Going

National Association of Social Workers. (1994). Declassification. In *Social work speaks: NASW policy statements* (3rd ed., pp. 74–78). Washington, DC: NASW Press.

Pecora, P. J., & Austin, M. J. (1983). Declassification of social service jobs: Issues and strategies. *Social Work, 28,* 421–426.

Saxton, P. M. (1988). Vendorship for social work: Observations on the maturation of the profession. *Social Work, 33,* 197–201.

Spaulding, E. (1991). *Statistics on social work education in the United States: 1990.* Alexandria, VA: Council on Social Work Education.

Specht, H., & Courtney, M. (1994). *Unfaithful angels: How social work has abandoned its mission.* New York: Free Press.

Tourse, R. W. C. (1995). Special-interest professional associations. In R. L. Edwards (Ed.-in-Chief), *Encyclopedia of social work* (19th ed., Vol. 3, pp. 2314–2319). Washington, DC: NASW Press.

Williams, L. F. (1987). Professional associations: Special interest. In A. Minahan (Ed.-in-Chief), *Encyclopedia of social work* (18th ed., Vol. 2, pp. 341–346). Silver Spring, MD: National Association of Social Workers.

Williams, L. F., & Hopps, J. G. (1990). The social work labor force: Current perspectives and future trends. In L. Ginsburg et al. (Eds.), *Encyclopedia of social work* (18th ed., 1990 suppl., pp. 289–306). Silver Spring, MD: National Association of Social Workers.

NASW MEMBERSHIP QUESTIONNAIRE

The following application form was in use prior to 1994.

NASW Membership Questionnaire

Personal

Title First Name M.I. Last Name	Sex ❏ F ❏ M
Street	Date of Birth
Second Line Street Address	Home Phone #
City State Zip Code	Office Phone #

Employment

Title
Employer
Street
City (Include Country, if foreign)   State   Zip Code

I would prefer to receive mailings at: Check one: Home ___ Office ___

There are NASW Chapters in all 50 states plus New York City, Metro Washington D.C., Europe, Puerto Rico, and the Virgin Islands. PLEASE NOTE that you will be assigned a chapter based on your mailing preference address unless another chapter affiliation is requested here. *I would prefer to be assigned to the _____ chapter.

Students
Date entered current degree program: (Month and Year) _____/_____
Expected graduation date _____/_____

Anticipated degree (BSW, BS, MSW, ETC.)	College or University/Division/ City & State	Major subject/ Program sequence

Education

Currently held degrees (List highest degree first)	Graduation Date Mo./Year	College or Universiy/ Division/City & State	Major Subject Program sequence

Ethnic Origin

☐ A. American Indian or Alaskan Native ☐ D. Chicano/Mexican American ☐ G. White

☐ B. Asian or Pacific Islander ☐ E. Puerto Rican (not Hispanic in origin)

☐ C. Black (not Hispanic in origin) ☐ F. Other Hispanic ☐ H. Other

Please check one ☐ new member ☐ former member (more than a year since renewing)

Regular Membership in NASW is open and limited to anyone who has received an undergraduate or graduate degree from a Council on Social Work Education (CSWE) accredited/recognized program.

Associate Membership is open and limited to anyone currently employed full time in the U.S. in a social work capacity (not self-employed or group private practice) who holds any accredited baccalaureate or greater degree, other than in social work. Associate members are not eligible for liability insurance and may not hold national office. However, national voting rights are extended after 5 years of continuous membership.

Retired/Unemployed/Doctoral Candidate Membership. Reduced dues rates are available to regular members who are retired or unemployed, i.e., totally unsalaried in any field, or to degree candidates in social work doctoral programs. In cases of temporary or extreme hardship, a reduction in dues may be requested.

Appendix 1

Student Membership is open to anyone currently enrolled in a Council on Social Work Education site-team approved, accredited or recognized degree program.

Prior Name (if previous member)
Prior I.D. No.

Applicants who hold a degree from a foreign university should call the Membership Records Department at the National Office for specific information on eligibility requirements.

Method of Payment—Please Check One:
❐ Check or money order payable to NASW ❐ VISA ❐ MasterCard

Card No._____Exp._____Amount $_____

Affirmation
I hereby affirm and agree that I will abide by the Code of Ethics of the association and agree to submit to proceedings for any alleged violation of the same in accordance with NASW bylaws. I further understand that falsification of the contents of this application will be grounds for rejection and/or termination of my association membership and revocation of any and all benefits resulting therefrom (see summary of code).

Signature_____ Date _____
CHECK, MONEY ORDER OR CHARGE CARD INFORMATION MUST ACCOMPANY THIS FORM.

Indicate your function in primary job and, if any, secondary job.

A. Direct Service (e.g., Casework Work, Clinical)	E. Consultant
B. Supervison	F. Research
C. Management/Administration	G. Planning
D. Policy Development/Analysis	H. Education/Training
	I. No Social Work Function
_____ Primary	_____Secondary

Indicate auspice of your primary job and, if any, secondary job.

A. Public Service—Local	E. Private and Nonprofit—Sectarian
B. Public Service—State	F. Private and Nonprofit—Non-Sectarian

C. Public Service—Federal
D. Public Service—Military

_____ Primary

G. Private for Profit; Proprietary

_____Secondary

Indicate setting of primary job and, if any, secondary job.
A. Social Service Agency/Organization
B. Private Practice–Self-Employed/Solo
C. Private Practice–Partnership/Group
D. Membership Organization
E. Hospital
F. Institution (Non-Hospital)
G. Outpatient Facility: Clinic/Health or Mental Health Center
H. Group Home/Residence

_____Primary

I. Nursing Home/Hospice
J. Court/Criminal Justice System
K. College/University
L. Elementary/Secondary School System
M. Employment in Non-Social Service Organization (e.g., business/ manufacturing; consulting/research firm; etc.)

_____Secondary

Indicate practice area of primary job and, if any, secondary job.
A. Children & Youth
B. Community Organizing/Planning
C. Family Services
D. Correction/Criminal Justice
E. Group Services
F. Mental Health
G. Public Assistance/Welfare

_____Primary

I. School Social Work
J. Services to the Aged
K. Alcohol/Drug & Substance Abuse
L. Developmental Disability/Mental Retardation
M. Occupational
O. Other (specify)_____

_____Secondary

Indicate the first and second practice commission with which you identify.*
A. Health/Mental Health Commission (e.g., Medical/Health Care, Mental Health, Disabilities, etc.)
B. Family and Primary Associations Commission (e.g., Children and Youth, Family Services, Services to the Aged, etc.)
C. Education Commission (e.g., Social Work in Schools, Colleges, etc.)

D. Employment/Economic Support Commission (e.g., Occupational Social Work, Assistance/Public Welfare, etc.)
E. Justice Commission (e.g., Corrections, Criminal Justice, etc.)

*NOTE: In 1985 NASW identified 5 fields of practice and established "5 Commissions" as an initial organizing framework for response to members' practice interests. The Justice Commission is not currently operational.

_____First

_____Second

Appendix 1

Indicate current annual salary (or self-employed income) from primary employment only.

☐ A. Under $10,000
☐ B. $10,000–14,999
☐ C. $15,000–17,499
☐ D. $17,500–19,999
☐ E. $20,000–24,999
☐ F. $25,000–29,999
☐ G. $30,000–34,999

☐ H. $35,000–39,999
☐ I. $40,000–49,999
☐ J. $50,000–59,999
☐ K. $60,000–69,999
☐ L. $70,000–79,999
☐ M. $80,000 & Over

The annual salary reported above is for:

☐ Full-time   ☐ Part-time

Indicate annual income from secondary employment, if any.

☐ A. Under $2,500
☐ B. $2,500–4,999
☐ C. $5,000–9,999
☐ D. $10,000–14,999
☐ E. $15,000–19,999
☐ F. $20,000 & Over

Indicate total years of social work experience since first social work degree.

☐ A. Under 2 years
☐ B. 2–5 years
☐ C. 6–10 years
☐ D. 11–15 years
☐ E. 16–20 years
☐ F. 21–25 years
☐ G. Over 25 years

NASW MEMBERSHIP APPLICATION

The following application form was developed in 1994.

NASW Membership Application

Your answers to the following questions will help us improve NASW Services to you and help us advocate for increased compensation. Your responses will be reported only in aggregate form. Please print.

Personal Information

1. Birth Date:_____mo/day/yr
2. Sex: Female ❏   Male ❏
3. Ethnic /racial origin:
   A. ❏ Native American (American Indian or Alaskan Native)
   B. ❏ Asian or Pacific Islander
   C. ❏ African American/Black (not Hispanic/Latino in origin)
   D. ❏ Chicano/Mexican American
   E ❏ Puerto Rican
   F. ❏ Other Hispanic/Latino
   G. ❏ White/Caucasian (not Hispanic/Latino in origin)
   H. ❏ Mixed Heritage
   I. ❏ Other (specify) _____
4. State social work license or certification?   Yes ❏   No ❏
   If yes, list state(s) and letter designation
   State_____
   Designation _____
5. List additional social work credentials:
   _____
   _____

6. Have you ever held elective public office?   Yes ❏   No ❏
   If yes, please specify: _____
   _____

7. Indicate current annual income.
   (Annual Salary or Self-employed Net Income)

Income	Primary Place	Secondary Place
A. Under $15,000	❏	❏

181

	Primary Place	Secondary Place
B. $15,000–19,999	☐	☐
C. $20,000–24,999	☐	☐
Income	Primary Place	Secondary Place
D. $25,000–29,999	☐	☐
E. $30,000–34,999	☐	☐
F. $35,000–39,999	☐	☐
G. $40,000–44,999	☐	☐
H. $45,000–49,999	☐	☐
I. $50,000–54,999	☐	☐
J. $55,000–59,999	☐	☐
K. $60,000–64,999	☐	☐
L. $65,000–69,999	☐	☐
M. $70,000–79,999	☐	☐
N. $80,000 & Over	☐	☐

8. Indicate total years of social work experience since first social work degree:

A. ☐ Under 2 years
B. ☐ 2–5 years
C. ☐ 6–10 years
D. ☐ 11–15 years
E. ☐ 16–20 years
F. ☐ 21–25 years
G. ☐ Over 25 years

9. Major Field of Practice

	Primary Place	Secondary Place
A. Aging	☐	☐
B. Child/Family Welfare	☐	☐
C. Criminal Justice	☐	☐
D. Health	☐	☐
E. Mental Health	☐	☐
F. Occupational SW/EAP	☐	☐
G. School Social Work	☐	☐
H. Other (specify)_____		
_____	☐	☐

10. Major Function

	Primary Place	Secondary Place
A. Administration/Management	☐	☐
B. Community Org./Advocacy	☐	☐
C. Clinical/Direct Practice	☐	☐
D. Policy Analysis/Development	☐	☐
E. Research	☐	☐
F. Supervision	☐	☐
G. Teaching	☐	☐

	Primary Place	Secondary Place
H. Training (agency-based)	❏	❏
I. Other (specify)_____		
_____	❏	❏

11. Work Setting

	Primary Place	Secondary Place
A. Business/Industry	❏	❏
B. College/University	❏	❏
C. Court/Justice System	❏	❏
D. Health—Inpatient	❏	❏
E. Health—Outpatient	❏	❏
F. Managed Care	❏	❏
G. Mental Health—Inpatient	❏	❏
H. Mental Health—Outpatient	❏	❏
I. Private Practice—Group	❏	❏
J. Private Practice—Solo	❏	❏
K. Residential Facility (group home, etc.)	❏	❏
L. School (pre-school–12)	❏	❏
M. Social Service Agency	❏	❏
N. Other_____		
_____	❏	❏

12. Type of Organization

	Primary Place	Secondary Place
Private		
A. For Profit	❏	❏
B. Nonprofit	❏	❏
Public/Government		
C. Federal, Military	❏	❏
D. Federal, Nonmilitary	❏	❏
E. State	❏	❏
F. Local	❏	❏

13. Work Focus

	Primary Place	Secondary Place
A. Alcohol/Drug Abuse	❏	❏
B. Dev./Other Disabilities	❏	❏
C. Employment-Related	❏	❏
D. Family Issues	❏	❏
E. Grief/Bereavement	❏	❏
F. Health	❏	❏
G. Housing	❏	❏
H. Income Maintenance	❏	❏
I. Individual/Behavioral Problems	❏	❏
J. International	❏	❏

K. Violence/Victim Services   ❏   ❏
L. Other (specify)_____
_____   ❏   ❏

14. Clients: Regardless of your setting, approximately how many people do you serve per year?_____

Please print.

Title (Mrs., Ms., Mr., Dr.)	First Name	M.I.	Last Name
Home Address			
City State Zip Code			
Country			
Home Phone Home FAX			

Does your employer pay your dues? Yes ❏   No ❏
Do you prefer mail sent to: Home ❏   Office ❏

Employment
Job Title
_____

Organization
_____

Organization Address
_____

City   State   Zip Code
_____

Work Phone   Work FAX
_____

Chapter Affiliation

Your chapter receives 50 percent of your dues to support its own programs. There are NASW chapters in all 50 states, plus New York City, Metro Washington, DC, Puerto Rico, the Virgin Islands, and International.

Note: You will be assigned a chapter based on your mailing address unless you request another chapter affiliation here:

_____

Appendix 1

Education

Currently held degrees (List highest social work degree first)	Graduation Date/Mo./Year	College or University City & State	Concentration

Attention Students

Anticipated Degree	Anticipated Graduation: Mo/Yr
College or University/Branch	
Concentration	Date Entered Program: Mo/Yr

For Office Use Only   School   Spec.   Mo/Yr   Lvl   CSWE

I.D. Category				

A956ab

Affirmation

I hereby affirm and agree that I will abide by the Code of Ethics of the association and agree to submit to proceedings for any alleged violation of the same in accordance with NASW bylaws. I further understand that falsification of the contents of this application will be grounds for rejection and/or termination of my association membership and revocation of any and all benefits resulting therefrom (see summary of code).

Signature _____ Date _____

NASW MEMBERSHIP DATA RECODING, 1991–1995 MEMBERSHIP SURVEY FORM

Question Area	Old Code	New Code
Ethnicity	American Indian or Alaskan Native	same
	Asian or Pacific Islander	same
	Black (not Hispanic origin)	same
	Chicano/Mexican American	same
	Puerto Rican	same
	Other Hispanic	same
	White (not Hispanic)	same
		Mixed heritage
	Other/Mixed heritage	other
Function	Direct Service	Clinical/direct practice
	Supervision	same
	Management/administration	Administration/management
	Policy development/analysis	Policy analysis/development
	Consultant	Other
	Research	same
	Planning	Policy analysis/development
	Education/training	Teaching
	No social work function	Other
Auspice	Public service–local	same
	Public service–state	same
	Public service–federal	same
	Public service–military	same
	Private not-for-profit sectarian	Private not–for–profit
	Private not-for-profit non-sectarian	Private not–for–profit
	Private for profit	Private for profit
Setting	Social service agency/organization	Social service agency
	Private practice—self employed	Private practice—solo

Question Area	Old Code	New Code
	Private practice partnership/group	Private practice—group
	Membership organization	Other
	Hospital	Health—inpatient
	Institution (non-hospital)	Residential facility
	Outpatient facility	Health—outpatient
	Group home/residence	Residential facility
	Nursing home/hospice	Residential facility
	Court criminal justice system	Court/justice system
	College/university	same
	Elementary/secondary school	School (pre-school–12)
	Non–social service organization	Other
Practice Area	Child & youth	Child/family welfare
	Community organizing/planning	Other
	Family services	Child/family welfare
	Corrections/criminal justice	Criminal justice
	Group services	Other
	Medical/health care	Medical/health care
	Mental health	Other
	Public assistance/welfare	Other
	School social work	School social work
	Services to the aged	Aging
	Alcohol & drug abuse	Other
	Developmental disabilities–mental retardation	Mental health
	Other disabilities	Other
	Occupational	Occupational
	Other	Other
Annual Salary	Under $10,000	Under $15,000
	$10,000 – $14,000	Under $15,000
	$15,000 – $17,499	$15,000 – $19,999
	$17,500 – $19,999	$15,000 – $19,999
	$20,000 – $24,999	same
	$30,000 – $34,999	same
	$35,000 – $39,999	same
		$40,000 – $44,999
	$40,000 – $49,999	$45,000 – $49,999
		$50,000 – $54,999
	$50,000 – $59,999	$55,000 – $59,999
		$60,000 – $64,999

Appendix 2

Question Area	Old Code	New Code
	$60,000 – $69,999	$65,000 – $69,999
	$70,000 – $79,999	same
	$80,000 and over	same
Experience	Under 2 years	same
	2–5 years	same
	6–10 years	same
	11–15 years	same
	16–20 years	same
	21–25 years	same
	over 25 years	same

INDEX

A

Academy of Certified Social
  Workers (ACSW), 14, 38,
  39
Adoption Assistance and Child
  Welfare Act of 1980, 9
Advocacy, 156, 165
Age
  date of highest degree and,
    49–52
  gender and, 47–48
  general data for, 25
  primary auspice and, 72
  primary function and, 115
  primary practice area and, 109
  primary practice setting and,
    87
  secondary function and, 124
  secondary practice area and,
    112
  secondary practice setting and,
    97
  shifts in, 48–49
  trends related to, 154–155
Americans with Disabilities Act
  of 1990, 9

Anti-Drug Abuse Act of 1988, 9
Associate membership, 4
Auspice, 33–35, 169. *See also*
  Primary auspice; Secondary
  auspice

B

Bureau of Labor Statistics (BLS)
  studies, 2, 4–5

C

Clients seen, number of, 38
Council on Social Work Education (CSWE), 4, 7, 154

D

Declassification, 158, 159

E

Education level
  age and, 49–52
  date of highest degree and,
    59–60
  ethnicity and, 54–56
  gender and, 44–46, 59

THE AUTHORS

Margaret Gibelman, DSW, ACSW, is professor and director of the doctoral program at the Wurzweiler School of Social Work, Yeshiva University, New York. She teaches in the areas of social welfare policy, management, and child welfare. She also has taught at Rutgers University and The Catholic University of America.

Dr. Gibelman has worked in human services as a clinician, supervisor, educator, and manager. In the latter category, she has served as executive director of the National Association of School Psychologists and the Lupus Foundation of America. She was also associate executive director of the Council on Social Work Education, the accrediting body for social work education programs in the United States.

Dr. Gibelman frequently consults with nonprofit organizations and is a senior consultant for the Council on Accreditation of Services to Families and Children. She is a frequent contributor to scholarly journals on nonprofit management, privatization, professional education, health care financing and policy, women's issues, and service delivery systems, and she is the author of several books.

Philip H. Schervish, PhD, is associate professor and chair of the research sequence, Howard University School of Social Work, Washington, DC. He has practiced social work as manager, researcher, policy analyst, and instructor since 1971. He holds an MBA and a PhD in social work. After serving six years as a legislative analyst and program evaluator for the Indiana General Assembly, he taught at Indiana University School of Social Work and The Catholic University of America School of Social Service.

Dr. Schervish's past research includes a national study of just compensation, models for redefining poverty in the United States, information use by social workers in mental health settings, and multicriteria decision support systems. He assisted in the development of a university-based social work curriculum in the former Soviet Union. His current research interests focus on information technology applications in the human services for decision support, distance learning, and social policy development with a social justice perspective.

WHO WE ARE: A SECOND LOOK

Cover design by Anne Masters Design
Interior design by Naylor Design, Inc.

Composed by Toni L. Milbourne and Patricia D. Wolf,
Wolf Publications, Inc., in Sabon and Stone Sans

Printed by Automated Graphic Systems on 60# Williamsburg
Smooth Offset

LEARN MORE ABOUT SOCIAL WORK WITH INFORMATIVE BOOKS FROM THE NASW PRESS

Who We Are: A Second Look, *by Margaret Gibelman and Philip H. Schervish.* Uses the 153,000-member database of the National Association of Social Workers to take a second look at who social workers are. Invaluable resource for scholars, labor force specialists, policymakers, and planners, as well as educators and practitioners.
ISBN: 0-87101-261-8. Item #2618. Price $27.95

What Social Workers Do, *by Margaret Gibelman.* Offers practical information about jobs available in specific service areas, the spectrum of social work roles and functions, the nature of social work practice, and best career bets for the future. An excellent introductory text, high school or college career planning guide, or professional career development manual.
ISBN: 0-87101-242-1. Item # 2421. Price $34.95

Study Guide for ACSW Certification, 4th Edition, *by Ruth R. Middleman.* Reviews the entire process for the Academy of Certified Social Workers (ACSW) and describes the certification examination for this most widely recognized and respected social work credential. The 4th edition contains newly updated questions for the examination. Licensing candidates and professionals preparing to take any standardized test will find it useful.
ISBN: 0-87101-264-2. Item #2642. Price $15.95

Legal Environment of Social Work, *by Leila Obier Schroeder.* Explains how the law affects the organization of social agencies and the delivery of services within complex organizations. Chapters highlight new legislation such as the Americans with Disabilities Act.
ISBN: 0-87101-235-9. Item #2359. Price $34.95

(Order form on reverse side)

ORDER FORM

Title	Item #	Price	Total
__ Who We Are	Item 2618	$27.95	_____
__ What Social Workers Do	Item 2421	$34.95	_____
__ Study Guide for ACSW, 4th Edition	Item 2642	$15.95	_____
__ Legal Environment	Item 2359	$34.95	_____
		Subtotal	_____
	+ 10% postage and handling		_____
		Total	_____

❏ I've enclosed my check or money order for $ _____.

❏ Please charge my ❏ NASW Visa* ❏ Other Visa ❏ MasterCard

_____ _____

Credit Card Number   Expiration Date

Signature _____

Use of this card generates funds in support of the social work profession.

Name_____

Address _____

City _____ State/Province _____

Country _____ Zip _____

Phone _____ _____

NASW Member # (if applicable)

(Please make checks payable to NASW Press. Prices are subject to change.)

NASW PRESS

NASW Press
P.O. Box 431
Annapolis JCT, MD 20701
USA

Credit card orders call
1-800-227-3590
(In the Metro Wash., DC, area, call 301-317-8688)
Or fax your order to 301-206-7989
Or e-mail nasw@pmds.com

Visit our Web site at http://www.naswpress.org   WWA2ND96